God's
COVENANT

Illuminating the Path to Your Calling

A DIVINELY ORDERED LIFE SERIES | VOLUME 2

DEBBIE N. GOLDBERG

SMOAKHOUSE PUBLISHING

Smoakhouse Publishing
1313 Mockingbird Rd
Key Largo, FL 33037
www.smoakhousebooks.com

Ordering Information:
Quantity sales. Special discounts are available on quantity purchases by corporations, associations, and others. For details, contact the publisher at the address above.

Printed in the United States of America

Library of Congress Cataloging-in-Publication Data
2017944913

Goldberg, Debbie N.
A Divinely Ordered Life Series, Volume 2
God's Covenant: Illuminating the Path to Your Calling / Debbie N. Goldberg
ISBN 978-0-9983227-1-1
1. Self-Help : Religion & Spirituality 2. New Age & Spirituality : Mental & Spiritual Healing 3. Practices & Sacred Texts : Unitarian Universalism

Book design by Elena Reznikova

Second Edition

These books are a gift of love from Spirit.
They are a guide for your spiritual journey.
This volume provides an opportunity for you to gain a deeper connection to Spirit and your calling. Your journey will take courage, complete honesty, openness, and patience. You will need compassion, faith, persistence, and a commitment to your self to create a loving purposeful life.

About the Author

Debbie N. Goldberg practiced as a clinical therapist for eighteen years in Pennsylvania specializing in mental health and substance abuse issues for adults and couples. She has worked in a variety of settings and is now in private practice as a Spiritual Mentor residing in Islamorada, Florida. She brings the spiritual knowledge of her own awakening into her work to inspire healing, love, joy, purpose and creativity as each of us works through our own spiritual journey.

Acknowledgements

(Dedications, Acknowledgements, Preface & Background
for the book series *A Divinely Ordered Life*)

In Volume 1, *Are you ready to listen? –God*, I acknowledged all those who have been part of my spiritual journey and who have touched these books in preparation for their release. I also included background information about myself and the circumstances that prompted me to travel my spiritual path. Please refer back to Volume 1 if you are interested in this information.

Contents

This book is a gift of profound love to you from Jesus. Through me, Jesus delivers a message to you that must be learned in order for you to live a life of happiness, gratitude, love, healing and purpose. This series of books have become my co-creation with Jesus and God. I pray blessings to you that these books bring you to a place of co-creation of your life's purpose.

*God – Please bestow the blessings you
have bestowed onto me
to the readers of these books;
heal me and heal them.*

Chapter One

SPIRITUAL LOVE

Nothing can take your breath away
like feeling the love of God, your higher self and the
spiritual universe that resides within you...

Allow me to give back to you the gift of love,
the secret of life and your Divinity.
Walk with me through the pages of these books
to find your true self and joy.

"We love you, you are a blessing and you are blessed. You are a beautiful light of God." Can you imagine hearing that every single day? You could if you discover how to listen to Spirit within you.

This series of books is called *A Divinely Ordered Life* and it describes the framework of God's Covenant (agreement) with our soul. God's covenant is that you will awaken and remember who you truly are and realize your oneness with God. The Spiritual journey is your soul's return Home to love, peace and joy. Your higher purpose is unity with God and fulfilling the promise of your agreement, your Divine calling, your co-creation with God. This has nothing to do with what type of job or career you have.

Each one of you has your own very special journey that is unique to you. You come to earth as a divine being of goodness. You are connected to and are a part of the energy of the cosmic universe. That cosmic energy resides within your heart. You come well equipped since this energy is fueled by God's unconditional love and an intuitive spiritually guided navigation system that endows you with the ability to love, create, and express joy. In this existence you take on a human form and those human characteristics enable you to feel and experience life fully, both negatively and positively.

Life is full of karmic lessons to learn and challenges to overcome. I discussed in Volume 1, *Are you ready to listen?-God*, how your soul discussed with God what lessons you are to learn during your current lifetime. You also have a higher purpose to actualize.

I believe that your soul actually picks you, your parents and all of the other people in your life who are destined to play supporting roles to help you learn your lessons and achieve your dreams. What if that's true?

2

Think about it. Think about the people in your life, past and present, some of them may have been wonderful and some may have been horrible. Think about what karmic lessons each of them might have been trying to teach you.

Most of life's challenges stem from energetic patterns that can be traced back to past lives and past experiences. We also absorb some of this energy, these patterns of thought and belief, from the society in which we live. For example, each society has its own ideas about things such as: what constitutes 'success'; what constitutes beauty; what does love look and feel like; what value should we assign to money and wealth. Think about all of the ways that our thoughts, beliefs, and perceptions are molded by our society, and perhaps more importantly, by the position we occupy within that society.

Much of this energy, both positive and negative, is also generationally transmitted. It has been passed down to you through your family from one generation to the next. Take a moment and think about some of the basic ideas about life that you grew up with that you learned from your parents, grandparents and other members of your extended family. If you know anything about your family history (your family story) you can probably even see where/how these ideas originated and how they were passed down from one generation to the next until they were finally passed down to you.

Many of these energetic patterns are expressed through our ego and are the foundation for many of the destructive behavioral patterns and patterns of thoughts, feelings and beliefs that need to be healed (disbelieved) and overcome. Most of life's problems and challenges can be traced back to the influence of the human ego and generationally transmitted energy.

The human ego is a tremendously powerful spiritual energetic component that is designed to help you in your spiritual journey through this human experience. The trick is to understand the apparent contradiction that the ego helps you by throwing up one roadblock after another in your life. It doesn't sound very helpful does it? But the purpose of all of those roadblocks and challenges that you are experiencing is to show you the opposite of the true nature of the divine spiritual being that you are. It sounds counter-intuitive, but in some very fundamental way, you can't really understand and appreciate what is good without seeing and experiencing what is bad.

Your ego projects negativity and creates the illusion that you experience as your physical life on earth. It deceives you by creating all of the misconceptions that create so much of the energy-draining drama that wastes your time. At the same time, your soul is projecting all of the beauty around you. Understanding the role that your ego plays in your life and your spiritual journey is absolutely essential if you are to learn all of your spiritual life-lessons and grow your heart with love and compassion for your-self and for all mankind.

Your job then is to subdue your ego, gain mastery over it, and then evolve it into a state of higher consciousness with you through love. Actually, it is more like the melding of our humanity and the Divine rather than seeing it as separate. The goal is to heal this separation and evolve your soul to the point where you remember who you truly are, a divine spirit of love and light having a human experience. Our Divinity and humanity are inexplicably entwined.

The power that you have to create is tremendous. You have a universe of God's love supporting you and helping you to succeed. We each have a Spiritual Master within as well as many Spiritual guides. You are never alone. You never go through your Spiritual awakening alone or life for that matter. You need to go inside yourself and seek this Spiritual Master because each of you has your own special course of Spiritual instruction. It is designed just for you.

Your soul is already anchored, grounded, and rooted in God and has everything you will need for your journey. This is why you need to look inward before relying on outside sources and remedies all the time.

You succeed by aligning with your true calling or purpose in life, and creating expressions of l
You have earthly dreams, but it is your Div
that are always higher and take priority. Wher

into alignment with your Divine purpose, you then get to live the dreams of your life through the joy of creating through love. This is your soul's fulfillment of its covenant with God.

You could look at this as if your life is an airplane journey and you are the pilot. God is in the control tower and the whole Spiritual universe, including your soul, is your co-pilot. You are working on your flight plan to take you to any destination you want to go. Your flight plan is formed by your thoughts, beliefs and feelings.

Although you are in the pilot seat, God and the co-pilots are always guiding you as the navigation system through your body and heart, even though you may not be aware of this. This autopilot system is always on. God and you always have the last say since you are co-creating.

As you land and check out destinations along the way, you may change your mind (your flight plan) as you get new creative ideas. As you come more into alignment with your calling, you may find that Spirit guides you to consider other destinations.

Many of us get stuck at the first or second destination and then we limit the experiences we could be having and what we came here to do. We get stuck because our egos have burdened us with too much negative heavy baggage. We may be afraid to keep flying.

Understand that you are loved and chaperoned ḥroughout your whole life. You are safe and have everything you need for this journey. You lack nothing. All you need to do is raise your consciousness and expand your awareness and it sparks your awakening.

The fascinating part of this is that the physical reality that you experience is an illusion, like a virtual reality. Your soul and ego are creating all of the projections that you see as life. Nothing is real, although it feels very real. Actually, the only real thing is the vibration of love. You are simply pure energy and so is everything else. Your challenge is to keep creating love and joy through your own uniqueness without letting the illusion of life keep pulling you back into believing that it is real. Because our energy is one, from God or Source, which ever you prefer, we are all energetically connected to everything in life. Our souls are collectively sharing this human experience together, collectively evolving to new and higher levels of consciousness.

I will be using the term God since that is what I call the source of love in this universe. You may replace God with Spirit, Universe, Source, Chi, Buddha or any other word or name that resonates with you more. It is all a description of love.

Chapter Two

INTOXICATING UNCONDITIONAL LOVE

You are deeply blessed
and it is time for you to collect your blessings...

When I first started hearing the messages I described in chapter one, it came from Jesus and other Spiritual entities over a period of 2½ years. Hearing that I was so loved daily was very reassuring to me and for a long time brought me to tears. Yet I struggled to believe it. I was overwhelmed by the intoxicating unconditional love that I very much needed to hear and feel. This Spiritual love was so great it took my breath away.

Thy Will Be Done.
I am dedicated to the cause of promoting the
Reign of God within our hearts
To Love, Cherish, & Honor Ourselves and Others

I prayed to stay connected and never wanted to be apart from this love. Starting in September 2014, I would ask, "Jesus, God what do you want to share with me today? Please bless my clients and me to have a healing therapy session and to bring them to the light and love as you have done for me, please awaken them and lead me." Then I would write in my day-timer whatever short but powerful message was given to me. It was a great way to start. I passed the guided imagery technique I learned through Inner bonding along to my clients and immediately started to receive positive feedback that it was very helpful for them as well. They loved connecting with their Spiritual guidance.

Initially, many of the messages I received were about the importance of taking better care of myself. I understood what these messages meant. I had been consciously failing to acknowledge the effect that working too many hours and not enough balance in my life was having on me both physically and mentally. My day started at 5:15 a.m. After getting myself ready to face the day, I had a 40-minute drive to work. I would return home by 7 p.m. completely exhausted; but that didn't stop me from doing more work. Luckily, my husband would help with dinner, would clean up afterwards and was generally very understanding about my long days. If I were not doing paperwork in the evening I was in a trance watching a soap opera on TV or surfing the internet simply as a way to numb myself. I spent time with friends on the weekend, tried to catch up on chores or shopped, but again, much of the shopping was just another way to numb myself and avoid having to acknowledge and confront the lack of balance in my life. At the time, I had very little insight into what I was doing. I was on "go" mode. I had to be doing something all of the time, even if it was wasting time on something.

My issue was, I had no idea how to take care of myself, how to self-sooth with love and compassion or how to nurture myself emotionally, physically or spiritually. I resisted taking good care of myself. I would feel guilty if I took time just for me. In reality, I was telling myself I was not worth it. I was always putting myself on the back burner.

I was unconscious of the fact that I had been operating at a high level of anxiety that produced all of the vast energy that I poured into my work. I also didn't recognize that all of this anxious energy was being stored in my body with extremely negative consequences. In retrospect, I was an adrenaline and cortisol junkie and I now recognize that this had been going on for most of my life. These chemicals took over my world and made me feel like I had to go from one thing to the next without ever slowing down to really take care of myself. It was my way of disconnecting from myself, and my ego was a willing taskmaster. It was all an elaborately constructed distraction to shield me from having to stop, look deep within myself and deal with the realities or delusions of what was to be found there.

What I thought was good for me was not. For years I would go to jazzercise class because I love to dance, but that would get my heart rate up. I had already been operating at such a high level of intensity every day that when I went to jazzercise my heart rate would soar to around 200 beats per minute and my head would feel like it was going to blow off. Eventually my knees gave out. I had driven myself too far. It seemed like a real setback at the time. But looking back on it all now, I see that perhaps this was a good thing because it made me stop and confront the reality of what I had been doing to myself. I began to see my patterns of going through seasons of intense focus, over-exercising and eating a very restrictive diet, followed by periods of a lack of focus, lack of exercise and having an unhealthy diet.

In reality, what happened was that my soul intervened because I wasn't seeing my life clearly. Yes, you heard me right, our very soul can use pain to get our attention, or shut us down physically to protect us from completely imploding. Most of us still don't listen. Most of us really don't know how to listen. We just keep going day after day stuck in our same old harmful and limiting patterns. We have to recognize that everything that is happening to us is a lesson, including physical pain. Physical pain is stuck energy and resistance to dealing with our feelings.

As a result of my soul's intervention, I began to slow down and eventually began to meditate. It took me about a year or so to develop a practice of meditation that brought me to deeper understandings. Each day as I quieted my mind and meditated I heard that I needed to work on my health, to eat better, to exercise through slow dance, and simply take time to slow down. I had to learn how to lower the anxiety and stress that kept the elevated levels of cortisol and adrenaline running amok inside me. Deep breathing became my best friend. Breath work is extremely healing.

At first, I experienced a lot of resistance to listening to my higher self. This resistance comes from the ego and from old emotional wounds that have yet to be fully processed, healed and integrated. Resistance is not unique to me. Anyone walking a spiritual path understands the resistance to obeying one's higher self that our ego generates. This resistance causes us to experience a lot of pain and grief. I would get so frustrated and annoyed with myself for not following through with what my higher self was recommending.

The ego is always projecting separation within us as if our higher self is a separate entity. This is part of the illusion that keeps the ego in control. There is no separation, we are one, we are whole. We are made as God intended us to be, a mixture of Divine and human. In fact, in volume 3, I will talk about what I have been shown spiritually about the double helix of our DNA. One strand is for our Divinity and the other is our humanity and they are fused together as one purposefully.

It feels as though we are going through an emotional war at times as our higher self and ego fight for control. For most of my life I didn't realize there was a spiritual war going on within me. The ego wanted to keep me in a stressed-out trance, my mind filled with work, family worries and self-judgment. This had become my norm. My soul wanted me to awaken, find my spiritual, physical, and emotional balance and evolve into the person I was meant to be.

In 2015, I was given a directive from my higher self to cut back on my work schedule. It seemed that this was a pretty drastic course to follow. I would have to cut back on clients and of course it would affect my income significantly. Although I was fearful and worried about it I obeyed. I was told to have faith that everything would be okay and that I needed to quiet my fears and listen. When I felt fearful I was encouraged to reach out to my higher self and talk about what was scaring me. While part of me was fearful, another part was excited and relieved to slow down.

It was an important step in my spiritual path that allowed me to experience what life was like at a slower pace, to learn better self-care, and to increase my commitment to this process. The end result has been the writing of these books, and the discovery of a new career. I am learning how to be me. Of course I couldn't see all of that when I first started down this path, but I now understand that being confronted by all of my fears and anxieties that came along with changing my career was really a lesson that I needed to learn about building faith and trust within God and myself.

The quest for self-love and coming to a place where you can give yourself what your heart truly needs can seem like a remarkably long journey. That's why it is so important that you make a strong and unshakable commitment to your own personal spiritual journey and to the process that will allow you to reach your goal. Nothing else is more important than taking care of you. No one knows what is best for you more than your higher self and spiritual guides. They know your spiritual curriculum.

Chapter Three

EVERYTHING YOU NEED IS WITHIN

Explore yourself. Find your essence,
and celebrate who you truly are.
You are the gift…

Reaching inside of you to find all the support you need is a quest with amazing surprises around every corner. There is more loving spiritual support available to help you evolve your soul than you could ever imagine. That support comes to you from God. Look at it as having your own coaching staff with each coach focused on teaching you a different lesson and providing you with a different type of support. Most of us don't realize that we have access to this vast network of support, but as I stated in the first book, God's kingdom (Universe) is within us, and always has been.

You will expand your ability to access this kingdom

as you grow spiritually and become ready to attain the next level of consciousness. It would be too much for you to handle if everything were accessible to you all at once. It takes time to practice and integrate the knowledge and wisdom you have started to acquire.

Experiencing the initial stages of spiritual awareness and growth can be overwhelming. As you begin to open your eyes and heart you are like a sponge absorbing all of this new information. Much of it is completely opposite of that which you have previously understood about life or yourself.

It may take quite a while to integrate it all; in fact it may take a lifetime. You have to give yourself some time each day to be quiet and reflect on the wisdom you are receiving. If you don't, it will be more difficult to integrate the wisdom into your heart and put it into practice. At times, it has taken me six months to a year to understand a single concept or truth. Once I begin to understand the concept, I get to see it operating in my life at different levels of awareness over and over again. Each time a lesson is revisited I am able to see it at a much deeper and more expansive level.

Your spiritual guides and higher self are always there to help you reflect on the wisdom you are learning and to help answer your questions. Ask your spiritual guides or higher self to help you find the answers that are already there inside you. Some of us receive our spiritual messages in images. It's perfectly normal to have questions and need help since we are coming from a place controlled by our ego and our programing that has no awareness or insight about truth, light or love.

There will be a period of time when you will seek answers outside of yourself, and that's okay. That's why you are reading this book. We look for reassurances and validation that we are on the right path. We find other seekers on their own journey, and it helps us feel better that we are not the only one working through this difficult unknown process. In fact, the universe is set up to send us these reassurances and they show up at exactly the right time and exactly when needed.

There are a number of fabulous programs offered around the world that can aid in raising our consciousness or help us in our spiritual journey. Unfortunately, not everyone has the time or the financial wherewithal to access and take advantage of these resources. Whether you are able to take advantage of these programs or not, please understand that the most important resource that is available to you comes from your own spiritual guides that you access by going inside, by seeking and looking within.

When I awoke, my thirst for information to help me understand what I was experiencing was insatiable. I discovered volumes of programs, techniques, books, and meditations, and was fascinated by all of it. I signed up for email messages so I could tap into the wealth of information that is available through the internet. Every new thing I found looked better than the last and I was fascinated by the excitement and stimulation of learning. A whole new world opened up to me that I had not discovered before.

Each day, I felt as though I had embarked on a treasure hunt. Each day, I felt as though I was uncovering new treasures. This excitement and exhilaration is normal but it also resulted in my receiving an onslaught of daily emails and messages that I didn't have time to absorb. It became overwhelming for me and really started to make my head spin.

We are so used to looking outside ourselves for everything we forget to look inside. In my meditations, I kept hearing that I needed to seek within and limit what I did on the outside. We can become so focused on other peoples' light and knowledge that we forget that we have our own light and knowledge within. Basically, we all have access to the same knowledge within each of us. We simply have to tap into it. So, the important message here is that if you want to engage in a program or utilize some external resource, that's wonderful. Just don't let it keep you from your most important work, which is meditating and seeking from your spiritual guide within.

This is another reason I am writing this series of books. They can serve as a kind of self-help guide to which you can always refer whenever you might need them. Over time, you will come to realize that you never have to look outside yourself for answers since all the wisdom you'll ever need about you, your life, your specific spiritual curriculum and purpose is already within you and readily available to you every moment of the day.

This doesn't mean that we don't need help from others or that others can't be helpful to us. We all need to support each other in a variety of ways, and I readily admit that I don't have all of the answers. I too have fallen victim to forgetting this and have been hijacked by my ego to keep looking outward for guidance. Inward is always the answer!

I have also had beautiful teachers who helped me learn amazing things and I am extremely grateful for all of their wisdom and help. But everyone has her/his own beliefs about life and walking the spiritual path. It can be confusing when what you are learning from external sources is different from the guidance you are receiving from within.

Until you become comfortable and trust the process, you will keep looking to others to provide answers for you. At times, we resist going inside or somehow forget the importance of tapping in to your spiritual guides. Sometimes, you simply think that you can do everything on your own. This is normal. Have patience with your self. For most of us, the only knowledge we have about the spiritual world is whatever generational or societal programing we've grown up with, so it's easy to look to others for answers.

Most of us have not been given a Spiritual framework to use for walking a Spiritual path. Truth be told, each of us has our own unique path to walk so they will not be the same. We get drawn to different things. Remember, there's no date by which your goal must be achieved; it's a journey.

The need to look beyond our selves for answers is all part of an important lesson...we all want immediate gratification from the outside world and we all lack trust in our selves. We've never learned to search through our heart. We have learned to look through our mental lens to rationalize and understand things. It's a lot to contemplate.

From day one we learn to rely on others for everything. We become dependent on others for our wellbeing...emotionally, spiritually, physically, and financially. Accepting the idea that our wellbeing can be created by us and comes from within us is an extremely important shift in thinking. Wellbeing is our Spiritual nature always. For most of us, it's a paradigm shift in the way that we think, but it's extremely empowering. The goal is to create a sense of safety within us, not outside of us. We need to believe in ourselves and learn to love ourselves. All is always well.

I spent much of my life relying on others to love me and take care of me emotionally because I didn't know how to do it myself, although I thought I did. Rather than caring for myself, I focused on what I thought other people needed and tried to take care of them. Most of us have not been taught emotional self-reliance in a healthy way. I could create financial security and some degree of physical safety for myself but I didn't know how to create my own emotional security or that it was my responsibility to do so.

I was always looking to others for approval, self worth, and validation and at times I still do this. I was always looking for someone to help me make choices because I never learned how to believe in myself. I learned that it was my job to validate me, not others. Everything I learned about me and about life came from my family and societal programing. Unfortunately none of it was correct. It really wasn't anyone's fault. My teachers were simply spiritually unconscious. Besides, the awakening would not be so sweet if it were not this way. God's unconditional loving validation for you sets the stage for this growth. This comes from a very deep connection within, and you have to be the one who keeps going inside to cultivate it.

Part of the resistance to accepting the fact that we create our own wellbeing is that it simply 'does not compute.' Our mind cannot grasp the profound spiritual truth we are learning because much of it does not seem to make rational sense on an earthly plane. We spend so much time resisting things that we don't understand.

We ask: "How can I stick this square peg into that round hole?" Spiritually, I am told I can do this, but I don't see how; I need to see it to believe it." Our ego programing contains a lot of black or white thinking and if it cannot see something or fit it into an acceptable context then there will be no understanding.

The spiritual journey is about learning to see and know life through your heart rather than your vision or mind. It is about developing deep trust and faith through eternal spiritual love and the infinite well of wisdom and light that flows within you. It is like putting on corrective lenses for the very first time.

We can't change our ego; it is what it is. But this leads us to the concept of faith, the fundamental, unshakable belief that there are things in the universe that cannot be proven, things so much bigger than ourselves that we cannot see or understand, and yet they do exist. Our ego is one of those things. It is part of our Divinely ordered life, it is Divinely orchestrated, and plays a tremendous role in our spiritual growth. The ego is part of us and always will be. We need to accept it and love it, but not listen to it.

In order to feel safe, our ego mind wants control over what we think, what we believe, what we do and how we see the world and how the world sees us. It does this by putting everything into a context that it understands. We have all had experiences where we thought we understood something, but then ultimately discovered that we did not understand it at all.

Many of us have had experiences for which there is seemingly no earthly explanation. It is extremely hard for our ego to accept that it doesn't know everything. As a result our ego will resist truths if it is unable to see 'how things work.' At the beginning of my spiritual awakening, I'd learn a new concept from my Spiritual guides and think, "I just don't get it. I can't see how that could be." Over time, I would learn a little more and then the pieces of the puzzle would start to come together. This is the process.

Journal Entry 1/17/2016
With Angel Simon

Me: *There are so many things that don't make sense.*

Simon: *I know. It will get easier with time. The more time you spend with us the more your knowledge will grow. It is not easy being human…so many tragedies, so much drama, pain, happiness, birth, and death. It is very complicated. It is important to remember not to rely on your thinking or understanding. If you consider life through a spiritual perspective it will be easier to look at everything as a planned lesson designed to help evolve your soul. Even past prophets succumbed to the ego. Everyone experiences times of doubt. It is nothing new. You expect so very much of yourself and it continues to pressure you.*

Me: *I see that I keep falling into the same trap of my patterns.*

Simon: *Yes, it will stop someday soon.*

Me: *I hope so, I will continue to work on staying present and connected.*

Simon: *You cannot fix anyone else either Deb. They have their own process to go through. Keep focusing on yourself. Blessings are coming, miles and miles of blessings.*

Me: *Thank you. Who am I talking to?*

Simon: *My name is Simon. I am one of your angels.*

Me: *You seem very sweet.*

Simon: *Thank you.*

Me: *I never heard of an Angel Simon before.*

Simon: *I know. There are many of us here trying to help you and everyone else.*

Me: *Thank you Simon. It is interesting how Spirits take turns working with us. I spend a lot of time with one and then someone else shows up and takes over, sort of a tag team!*

Simon: *Yes. I see that is how you look at it. We all have different lessons for you so it depends on where you are at the moment, what you need and what you are ready for.*

Me: *What is our time together about?*

Simon: *Reflection, my love, and that can be in many ways. Like the reflection of the bible story of being human, seeing your reflection in another person and in God.*

Me: *Yes, I see. What is it that you want to help me know or learn?*

Simon: *It appears that you are seeing different reflections within yourself. You see your positive attributes, how capable and responsible you are, how loved you truly are and the affect you have on others. It is beautiful how loving and caring you are. You also see all of your negatives, your faults, neediness, insecurity, etc. These are reflections of your ego, your wounded selves. They have nothing to do with your soul. Only the positive attributes reflect your soul. We need to start seeing the correct perspective and not the skewed one.*

Me: *How do I do this?*

Simon: *By remembering whom you really are. Remind yourself of how strong you are and how others see you as a positive influence.*

Me: *I just had a flashback of not being or acting that way many times.*

Simon: *Remember, you are also here to teach others lessons* *(unknowingly) that they need to learn as well. As an example, if you lose control of your emotions and others who are struggling with the same issue witness that, then you become a reflection of what they need to heal inside. You also learn from your own behavior. These behaviors do not define you or another person. This is just acting out and believing the drama of the mind, the storyline that people react to that affects them and others. So stick to reality, the truth of who you really are.*

Chapter Four

SEPARATION FROM THE EGO

All Souls Are To Be Set Free From
The Bondage Of The Ego

Your spiritual journey will take you to a point where you question who you are. I have come to understand that our spiritual growth leads us to make a direct connection with Spirit through our heart. This is how we build our internal relationship with our self and detach from ego and all of its human programing. To set the intention to connect to our guidance helps us to begin to separate from our ego. However small that separation might be, it's a great start. Separating from the ego is important because we have aligned with the ego and it is irrational. Here's the kicker. We separate from the ego at first but then need to reintegrate it into our being in a healthy manner through evolving it with our soul through self love. I know this sounds crazy but it appears to be the process.

It's important, if possible, to be able to access a visual image of your spiritual guides and I discussed how we achieve this in *Are you ready to listen?-God*, Volume1 of this series. Having a visual experience with your guidance gives us something to relate to. We experience it fully. We can see our guidance, hear it and know it in our heart. We now have a visual reference although we are not quite sure how it works, or how it happens, but still, we are experiencing it. We need to allow the images if they want to come. They are not scary.

Even though your ego does not want you to go inside, part of you knows that this is where you need to be and that you'll experience great love, joy, peace and contentment there. In fact, it is bliss. Once the wedge between you and your ego is now in place you will be able to continue to separate from your ego over time and find your highest, soul/spirit, and the universe that resides within. For me, Jesus first put the wedge into place. From that point onward, God, my higher self and other Spiritual guides also helped me bit by bit to increase the separation from ego.

The separation consists of discerning which voice is your ego's, then not listening to it, not believing it, or taking to heart anything it says about you or anyone else. This discernment takes a lot of practice since the ego plays several roles including a spiritual one. My ego acts like Jesus or my higher self at times and does a fairly good job of it. The only way I can discern who I am talking to is whether I feel peaceful or not. Ego does not create peace in us.

The first time I met my higher self was in a meditation that was led by Margaret Paul. It was in November 2014 when I was home sick for a whole week. I devoted that time to connecting to my spiritual guides. It was a powerful turning point for me since that is when I first heard God speak to me. I learned that my higher self is my pure spiritual self that feels and looks like love, God's perfection embodied. She is pure love and light. To me, my higher self looks like me, although angelic. Others have told me they experience their higher self as being without shape but that they can see something in the eyes that tells them it is their higher self.

I fell in love with my higher self. She became my best friend and knew everything about me, what I've experienced, what I need, what I want and where I am going. I really felt that my higher self and I became one. My higher self became my role model showing me who I am and who I will become. The love that I felt when I was in the presence of my higher self was so profound that I never wanted to leave her. During my meditations I found that I just wanted to be there with her in God's realm. When you see your higher self you are seeing your Spirit.

Awakening to the God Within

I give myself over to my highest, my soul,
the essence of who I am,
for She is the God within.
She is who carries the light of love, the torch,
the flame of my heart.
It is She, who carries on forever,
a beautiful Spirit of hope & joy,
a blessing to behold who bears witness to all
that She stands for, Divinity, & the Sacred.

I remember a meditation with my higher self when I was floating on a raft in a pool and she appeared right next to me also on a raft. We turned to each other and just gazed into each other's eyes. It was profound and I was instantly smitten by the love that came through her. I fell in love with her immediately. My higher self was teaching me how to fall in love with my self.

Even though I didn't really understand how or why this was all happening, I knew it felt right. I have never before felt the power of God's love shooting and coursing through my heart and veins like this. To me, it feels like a tingling Spiritual energy or vibration. I felt connected to the collective universal consciousness of Spirit's love.

As I continued to sharpen my ability to access my higher self through meditation, I discovered that my higher self appeared to me as different ages that were working on different lessons with me throughout the last couple of years. Early on, I copied them all, how they acted, how they dressed, how they wore their hair because it seemed to help me establish and solidify my connection with them. Once that connection is securely in place, you realize that your higher self is always (and always has been) talking to you and directing you.

As I progressed on this journey I learned that our higher self and we are one and the same, one perfect spirit, one perfect soul. In the beginning, she would tell me that we are one in the same over and over again but I saw her as a separate being because I could not see my true Divinity through my human eyes. Seeing my higher self was like looking at God. Our ego creates separation and will not accept that itself is Divine. Our ego wants to keep the separation between humanity and Divinity and there is no truth to this, we are all one.

You will come to understand that this is who you are; you and your higher spiritual self are one. The truth is, I'm still working on this myself. My higher self loves me and in joyously receiving that love I can then return that love to myself, specifically to the wounded and injured parts of me that were starving for recognition, love and attention. We all have a higher self to give us the love we need and to connect us to our own true divinity. In essence, you are feeling your own love, it is not separate.

Your higher self and all your Spiritual guides are the awesome team that transform you into the divine being you truly are, filled with the unconditional vibration of love and joy.

Your ego will continue to try to make sense of this experience by seeking information externally in the realm of human experience. For all of its efforts, it won't be able to do so. Still, it will never accept the truth that the spiritual part of you already knows. Your ego will do everything in its power to interfere as you try to meditate and connect with your higher self and your guides. Your ego is powerful but also can be very subtle at times. God has created a mighty ego to challenge us with contrast and it does an awesome job.

It's not always easy to distinguish between the soft inner voice of your spiritual guidance and the whispers of the ego that are subtly designed to sow seeds of fear and doubt. If you listen to your heart, if you listen closely, you'll soon learn to distinguish the sound of Spirit's inner voice, just as a baby instinctively recognizes the sound of its mother's voice. Follow the whispers of your heart, for it will bring you peace.

Connecting with your higher self is easy. During meditation, use your deep breathing and imagination to set the imagery in motion. See yourself in a beautiful place where you feel loved and safe. Ask your higher self to come to you and sit with you so that you can open your heart to her. Don't have any expectations. Just welcome whatever form comes to you. It will always be loving, so don't be afraid. If you feel fear, it's your ego interfering. Keep practicing until your higher self appears.

God understands that we will always search for meaning by trying to make sense of the external world outside of our selves. Remember, God also created the ego. As we grow spiritually, we will come to understand that He created the ego not to interfere with our spiritual growth but, when understood from a spiritual perspective, to be one of our most powerful spiritual teachers.

Of course our ego resists and can be down right nasty to your higher self. Mine was. My ego was not going to listen to my higher self and actually revolted against her for a very long time. My ego didn't understand who she was and did not want to give up control to her. My ego knew I was leaning towards listening to my highest and gradually weaning myself away from listening to it (ego) anymore. The clash between your ego and your higher self can create an enormous internal conflict, a kind of spiritual warfare.

My ego tried to make me think I was crazy, that there was no truth to my spiritual awakening. I went through a terrible time full of doubt, fear, and indecision, but in the end, my higher self won out. That's not to say that I still don't have moments of fear and uncertainty; I do. But as my connection to spirit grows stronger, those moments diminish in strength and duration. I'm on the right path.

The universe is set up to give us the reassurances needed to help us know that we are on the correct path to continue our journey toward spiritual consciousness. I look at it as a treasure hunt and search for clues in many different forms. Everywhere there are clues as to where to look or go to get closer to the treasure. That's what the reassurances are...to keep you moving forward on your journey of enlightenment and show you that you are on the right path.

As you do this and keep digging inward, you start to question everything you know. You start to understand that everything is an illusion and you begin to look at life differently. You ask yourself "Why didn't I see these things before?" It almost feels like magic, when you receive reassurances (it is all loving) and notice the small miracles and epiphanies happening in your life on a daily basis.

You begin to see truth in yourself and others. The truth you now see won't be the same truth you experienced before. You start to see and feel love everywhere. It's almost like falling in love with life and everyone and yourself. People give you smiles that you never noticed before. Favor comes your way from everywhere, even if it is something very small, some little thing that normally you would not have noticed. You sense that you are shifting to a higher level of consciousness and you feel gratitude for what you are witnessing.

The only thing that has changed is you! You are waking up and the spiritual growth you are experiencing is starting to subtly change you and open your heart. It's you that is different, whether you realize it or not, you are becoming present. As a result, you will begin to see all of the positive things happening in your life and you will affect everything around you in a more positive manner. It is an awakening, an amazing beautiful feeling and awareness.

You will start to see that things are not just as they appear to be. You start to feel as though you have some power to make things happen even though you don't understand it. This power comes from your heart opening and the resulting change in energy that you are now vibrating as you become more in alignment with the universe's vibration of love and joy. It feels magical, and the magic continues to grow as you go to higher levels of consciousness and keep expanding your heart and vibration to love and joy.

It is important to embrace all that is happening, for you are starting to see your own divinity and the power within your heart. It is as though a window were opened just a crack, just enough to let in a small sliver of the full awakening that could possibly be in store for you.

It will take time for that window to be fully opened.

Nevertheless, the glimpse you get from the opening you do see is spectacular. It fuels your passion to see and learn more, to keep digging deeper. You want to use your open heart to keep stripping away the illusion of the life that you knew and recognize that life now has a new meaning. This is what you see and this is what is meant by a Divinely ordered life. Everything has a different purpose and meaning to it then what you thought you knew.

This is exhilarating! You now can see and understand exactly how much God cares for you. It brings great peace to your heart to know that the whole Universe is there to support you. It also begins to rock the foundation of your ego. Ego is starting to lose its power. You recognize there is something so much greater than you.

You are graced with people showing up in your life, just at the right moment. Spirit angels are sent to help you take the next step. Sometimes these angels are people, new acquaintances, and sometimes they are people who you now see in a completely different light who have been near you the whole time. Powerful forces are at work within the universe to lead you to your purpose. Everything is divinely planned and believe it or not, the whole Universe lives inside each one of us.

Chapter Five

THE END GOAL

If you invite God to work in your heart
He will weave your soul like a fine tapestry
connecting all the imperfect threads
to create a beautiful Piece of Art...

The end goal is to align your will with God's will and to understand that you are one with God and your mutual purpose for your life. There are many starts, stops, and reversions back to old habits along this road. Each pause, each setback is designed to teach you lessons that will help you reach your ultimate goal.

When you begin to recognize all of the miracles in your life, it gives you a taste of what is to come. You don't mind hobbling down this spiritual road even if it is painful at times...and it is. You have to weed out all of the old programing, painful events and feelings you've experienced. You have to examine and acknowledge each one, feel the pain of them and then let them go. This means taking responsibility for all of your feelings, both negative and positive. It means that you stop blaming others, and that you forgive yourself and others. It means letting go of all of it, including attachments.

We are attached to many things that we think give us self worth or safety. In reality, we are simply giving away our power to those things or people that we think will give us the love, self-worth or safety that we so desperately seek. Or, alternatively, we use our resentments, pain and anger to justify our behaviors as we pursue the things to which we are attached. When we are able to shift our thinking from 'I need' (comfort, abundance, status, love, self worth) to 'I love and already have', then we have begun to honor and appreciate our self, other people, and everything around us in a much different way.

I already have all the things that I seek. Each of us brings with us into our earthly lives everything we could ever want or need. We have available to us all of the necessary power and resources we could ever need. If only we could come to fully appreciate and understand this, what an amazing world we would have.

Everything that has ever happened to you has been your own creation, the one that you decided on before you were born, (See Volume 1). I know that right now this is hard to digest, especially if you have had a lot of negative experiences in your life. Nevertheless, this is how you chose to learn the lessons for your soul's evolution. It took me a long time to take responsibility for this as well. We bring a whole host of Karmic lessons and energy with us into this world.

Remember, when you made these decisions, you were your soul/spirit. As a soul/spirit we know nothing of pain or suffering. The soul knows only love and joy, that it will never be harmed and that it does not die. When you made these decisions your soul knew that your life on earth would be an illusion, just as though you would be asleep and dreaming. Your soul understood that even though the experiences feel real, they are not.

After you were born into this world and as you grew older and experienced more of life, you began to disconnect from your soul and became attached to your ego as you experienced your first wounds. This is when the karmic lessons kick in. At birth, you forgot that you had already created a life path designed to confront you with lessons that you would need to learn in order to mature and strengthen your soul/spirit and reach higher levels of consciousness.

As you continue to grow in understanding, you will come to accept this. Right now, this may all seem very far-fetched because so many of us, including myself, carry life's battle scars from wounds that have cut and hurt us so deeply. We ask, why would I ever choose such a difficult life path for myself?

The truth is that what we are experiencing in life is actually a dream...or some of us might call it a nightmare. It is a dream that seems so very real, that takes a lot of convincing from Spirit to help us let go of the illusion that what we are experiencing is real. All that has happened, all that is happening in your life, has been the story in your dream and yes, it does feel real in every way, sense, shape and form. I will talk more about this in another chapter.

Journal Entry 2/27/2016
With Jesus

This conversation came about after my reading parts of 'A Course in Miracles' (ACIM) and assuming from the readings that the end goal is to reach a state where we let go of all human reactions or emotions other than love or joy.

Me: *So Jesus, something about 'A Course in Miracles' is bothering me; maybe I'm understanding it wrong. I know that in ACIM we are not supposed to be sad when someone dies because there is really no such thing as death. When someone loses someone dear to them how can we not be compassionate, how can we be so detached emotionally, after all we're still human? It feels callous to me not to have emotions, please help me understand this more.*

Jesus: *Debbie, this is a great question and I am glad you are coming inside with these questions. You are right, as a human being it would be very callous and uncompassionate to take an approach with others of 'Oh well, there is no such thing as death', or to say something like 'they are needed more as their spirit', or it is just their time to leave earth, or some such thing. I never meant ACIM to have someone be callous and forget that others are human and so are they.*

Me: *I feel like we should not have any emotions at all unless it is love or joy, is this wrong?*

Jesus: *This is difficult to understand. As a spirit there are no emotions, just joy, well, for the most part anyway. Because you are human you are going to experience other emotions, however, the job is to detach from all of the ego emotions coming from your old programing. It does not mean that nothing will ever upset you again.*

Me: *For example, say someone or my child gets hurt, it is so strange to think, 'well, that is their reality and their soul's path that is organized and planned therefore, they are not really hurt so I am not going to have any feelings about it.'*

Jesus: *I understand what you are saying and you are correct, the humanness in you should have feelings, it is part of your humility of being human. To transcend all emotion other than joy and peace you would not be human anymore, that would be difficult to achieve. That is not what my expectations are for you or anyone else. That is why we are writing a simple book.*

*A Course In Miracles is a book that was written by Helen Schucman in 1976. It was channeled through Jesus as a self-study curriculum for spiritual transformation. There are study groups all over the world.

The spiritual road is a toll road. There are tolls that we are required to pay such as, revisiting past pain, feeling current pain, and coming to grips with all of your faulty negative thoughts, beliefs and feelings produced by your ego that live in your shadow side/unconscious. You either pay the toll that allows you to access your treasure within and allows you and your Spirit to travel together to healing, or you don't pay the toll and you avoid the spiritual path altogether. Even if you choose to avoid the road right now, you will keep encountering people and experiencing events in your life that will confront you with the various lessons you are meant to learn. You cannot avoid it.

If you are reading this book, you have decided that you are ready and willing to pay the toll and begin to explore your internal truth. The toll being levied is your taking 100% responsibility for your perceived reality, for what you have created in the past and what you are currently creating in the present and the future.

Sometimes we're not ready to travel down a particular road and it's okay to come back to that one later. Some roads are easier to walk down than others when it comes to dealing with past painful events, and it is okay to start your journey by picking one of those easier paths. You have repressed your awareness of some roads, but they will appear at the right time for you when you are ready and strong enough to travel them.

As you travel down each path, you have to allow your feelings to emerge and feel them. You don't have to like them, but you need to accept them without judgment. As you get in touch with your feelings, take your spiritual guidance with you to walk the road together and follow each feeling or belief to its origin.

Let me give you an example from my own journey. I

have always judged myself harshly. I have always thought that I wasn't worthy, wasn't good enough, and that I had to do things to have someone like or love me. By the way, this is a very common belief. It is irrational and untrue and comes from old programing, negative experiences (trauma) and negative energy that have been passed down through your family from one generation to the next.

As I walked down that road to find the origin of this belief I came to understand that based on my childhood experiences, I felt that I was unworthy of love, inherently flawed and a disappointment. I felt that I couldn't do anything right to make anyone like me or make them happy. Because of these beliefs, I experienced a great deal of detachment from my self and others. I experienced fear, patterns of victimization, repressed anger, loneliness, emptiness and sadness.

I also recognized that I expressed all of these negative thoughts and feelings through anger and at other times submissiveness. I desperately tried to prove myself. I tried to be perfect. I was a workaholic, had feelings of entitlement, was detached from my self and others, had control patterns, and codependent behaviors. As I grew older I clung onto these patterns and beliefs. I unwittingly manipulated and controlled others and myself in order to gain whatever I thought I needed in order to satisfy my need for self-worth and love. I believed that I could not trust anyone else to help me with this. I felt truly alone with my needs and flaws. Much of this behavior was not in my awareness and happens when we are aligned with our ego.

This pattern of thinking affected all of my relationships in that I was projecting everything about my self onto others. The pattern affected my self-esteem, my career, and blocked me from my talents and gifts because I was always deeply fearful that I would succeed or would fail and be judged a disappointment or a fraud. Many of us live this way because we are spiritually unconscious, not having awakened to the truth of who we are, and having no idea we are going through life this way. We have blinders on.

We are constantly projecting everything from the past into the present. And the scary thing is that we are projecting not just based on the experiences of this lifetime, but upon the experiences from every incarnation we have ever lived. The energy of unhealed pain, unlearned lessons and untrue beliefs are following us from one incarnation to the next. This is what we are calling karma.

I spent much of my life doing more than I should for others. This codependent and workaholic behavior was my ego's attempt to keep my shadow side from others and from myself. I appeared capable, strong, responsible, but I was still living and seeing out of my smallness, my ego. I didn't allow for expansion into my divinity, so whatever riches internally there were for me to explore and expand went unnoticed and unused until I started to do this work. I didn't recognize that the performances I was giving of being capable, strong, and responsible were actually wonderful, positive attributes of mine. What I didn't realize is that I couldn't do all of those things for others unless the capability, responsibility and strength were integral parts of me as well.

In volume 1, I talked about our energetic set point and our ego's belief system. As I began to walk down my path non-judgmentally examining my thoughts and feelings, I came to realize that my energetic set point was sadness, aloneness, emptiness, grief and misery, and oft times being hyper from adrenaline and cortisol addiction. This was created by anxiety and stress. When we are stressed our bodies release adrenaline and cortisol that feels like energy, but is completely toxic to our body. We feel we can keep going, keep pushing ourselves with this energy and we do. But then these same chemicals keep us from sleeping or we sleep because we are exhausted. It's a vicious addictive cycle. It kills us slowly from the inside out.

When I was unconscious in my ego and alone, I was full of sadness, isolation, fear, anger and grief. I had repressed these feelings and kept them at bay by keeping busy with work and trying to prove that I was not a disappointment. I isolated myself from others and kept them at a distance. This was my coping mechanism for safety (although I was not unsafe). I was looking for other people and other things to fulfill the lack of love for myself and my empty love tank that always felt drained.

While I was engaged in my counseling practice and was helping others, I had good feelings because I was coming from a place in my heart that genuinely wanted to help others and was ultimately connected to my purpose. Yet even while I was counseling, I was essentially unaware and detached from my own self. These are all self-rejecting and self-abandoning behaviors. In truth, I was unknowingly an unhealed healer.

The therapist role gave me a good hiding place because it gave me a certain status and kept me enclosed in a somewhat rigid and structured environment, although I lacked any awareness that this was the case. I had very strong boundaries that allowed me to focus on others and detach from myself. It is interesting to now recognize that this dichotomy of helping from my heart and being detached from myself was present within me all the while. In some ways it represents the classic combination of the divinity and humanity (ego) present in all of us.

Another important revelation was that I didn't like to be at home. As I examined that feeling more deeply, I realized that when I was younger, my home was the source of this energetic set point. So as an adult "Home" became a negative and scary place where I didn't feel safe, I had to stay busy all the time. Unless I was outside of home working, I was stuck in my ego, traveling down this road day after day, year after year, feeling unsafe, uncomfortable and fearful at home, even though there was no truth to it! It was my poor little wounded selves that needed to be healed rising up in me (the vibrational energy that was trapped inside of me from many years of abuse).

Guess what else I figured out? These same feelings were also the unexpressed feelings of each of my parents. My parents were filled with their own uncomfortable feelings that they brought from their homes. What I was feeling was energy that was being passed down from one generation to the next.

When I looked at the rationale for my behavior, it didn't make any logical sense. At that period in my life, my home was safe. I had a loving husband. So why was I still projecting misery into my home as an adult? The answer is that the misery memory, the vibration, this energetic set point had played so long and so continually throughout my childhood, adolescent, teenage, and young adult years that it was now my set point even though my life was now totally different.

Look at it as repressed/suppressed energy and the only way to move beyond it was to heal the old wounds by re-feeling the feelings, processing those feelings, forgiving and freeing my self from their grip.

My nature is to be happy, upbeat and positive, so that's what other people saw. It was the 'acceptable' side of me that I was willing to share. I kept the shadow side of me from others and even from myself. I recognized that I needed to accept, acknowledge and take action by feeling the feelings I had as a child, understand where those feelings came from, process them and accept that my feelings were justified (whether rational or irrational) at that time in my childhood.

I have used Margaret Paul's Inner Bonding visualization technique that can be found on pg. 224, first paragraph, of her wonderful book '*Do I Have to Give Up Me to be Loved by God?*' It's a visualization technique that will put you in contact with your wounded inner child. It's a powerful tool that can help you begin the healing process. Why don't you try this technique with one of the negative patterns or beliefs that you keep seeing in yourself. This is how we learn to start taking responsibility for our feelings.

I wrote in my journal and gave my "wounded children" a voice to speak all the things that they wanted to say back then but couldn't. I wrote everything I heard from them with no holds barred, no editing. It gave me time to sort through the feelings; thoughts and experiences so I could be compassionate towards myself, process, forgive, and then let go. We are now ready to integrate that part of our self that we had abandoned. Journaling can be a very healing exercise in that it is very loving to your self and helpful in finding a way into your feelings and expressing them.

You are now ready to begin letting go of your feelings and stop creating experiences and reacting to them when they appear in your life. Example: if you have a core belief that you are going to be abandoned and rejected than you will unconsciously create events in your life that keep making you feel abandoned and rejected. If you've started to notice certain recurring patterns in your life, perhaps patterns within your relationships, this is how those patterns are being created. It shows how much creative power we have.

We create everything in our life, both the negative things and the positive. The positive beliefs must be strengthened and nurtured. The negative beliefs are simply not true. Once you are able to fully dissect and process them, you may even find that those beliefs have been passed down to you through your family and society. You may not have unconsciously created the negative beliefs yourself, but you may have inherited them, and they may be so strong that they are now a seemingly inextricable part of your emotional or psychological DNA. These irrational and debilitating negative patterns and beliefs have to be recognized, processed, and healed so the energy can be transmuted and defused. This happens when we stop believing and reacting to the irrational beliefs.

As we do this work, we are clearing out all of the transmitted energy that came along with us or was transmitted to us. We call this transmuting. When we are able to do this, it positively affects everyone else since we all participate in transforming a huge collective consciousness of energy.

Chapter Six

REVISITING OLD WOUNDS

Bare witness to what unfolds within you
Discover the magnificence that you are
Live the spark of the Divine that dances in your heart
You will forever be in awe...

Just use your imagination to see yourself at the age or ages when you experienced particularly painful events. Maybe you have a school picture to remind you of how you looked at that time. Use your imagination to sit and talk with your younger self. It is of the utmost importance that you approach your little self by being a loving adult filled with love and compassion as you talk about past events. See that younger self as your child. Imagine sitting them on your lap, stroking her/his hair, and expressing your love for them so they know you are coming from a place of genuine care.

These imagery tools are extremely useful and powerful and will lead you to healing. It is useful to have your spiritual guidance with you as you work through each visualization session. Recognizing that these wounded parts of you exist and repeatedly spending time with them will help dissipate reactions. Releasing the energy and feelings attached to past events can be a catalyst to healing and forgiveness.

Many times we reject or dislike ourselves at certain ages because we are not seeing the truth of who we are. We are seeing our self through the eyes of our extremely judgmental ego. We need to find compassion for that child and see them as innocent as through the eyes of God's/Spirit's love. You can never be completely healed until you are able to do this and re-feel your feelings with this child.

I found it easy to heal many of my wounded little selves, especially those who represented scars received at an early age. I also discovered that it was very difficult for me to express love and compassion for the wounded selves of age 5 and my teenage years. The same was true when I confronted my self at certain later stages in life such as age 21 and age 34. I didn't like myself at those ages and found it very difficult at first to be non-judgmental and attached. The resistance was palatable and came not only from me but also from those wounded parts of me that did not trust me to love or have compassion for them.

As I began to work with my teenage self, I felt shame

and guilt when I tried to process the trauma I experienced. In fact, I remembered how deep the isolation, sadness and grief was and how I just wanted to die at that time in my life.

My coping mechanism was seeking attention from boys, drinking, smoking pot, and being promiscuous at times. I just wanted to feel loved and was looking for something to soothe me and fill the emptiness that ached in my heart. The behavior of self-abandonment just caused more pain for me as the end result was 2 abortions by age 20. The first abortion was at age 18. I was sick all the time. I never thought that I could be pregnant until my mother asked if it were possible that I could be pregnant and whether that might be causing me to be sick. My mother ushered me to her ob-gyn and an abortion was performed, no questions asked. That was 1976. I was already detached from my self and now felt as though another nail had been driven into my coffin. I was alive but felt dead inside; I became part of the walking dead.

This experience added to my feelings of disregard. I felt that in the matter of my pregnancy, my feelings didn't matter and that I wasn't even given the time to let me try to understand what was happening within me. Based on what I had experienced up to that point in my interactions with others, I felt that life probably didn't mean very much. All around me I saw what appeared to be a blatant disregard and disrespect for life. Looking back on it now,

I don't know that it was the wrong decision to abort my pregnancy, but I do know that the decision was made out of my mother's fear of scandal and her concern for how having a child would affect my life.

By the time I was 20, I understood the drill that feelings didn't matter, so when I became pregnant again (using contraceptives this time) off I went for another abortion. I was hardened and cared little about myself or anyone else by then. I felt like a disregarded entity and I treated myself and other people accordingly. My focus was on what I needed to do in order to feel safe and loved. I lacked a strong set of ethics and morals in my relationships throughout my 20's and 30's. All of my repressed pain was resonating in me and I continually sought to bury and suppress my true feelings. The grief I was carrying was so heavy it weighed me down most of my life and I never acknowledged that it was there.

As I look back now upon those difficult times it's interesting to see that my soul was focused on trying to love my family, doing good work, being successful and moving forward while at the same time my ego was dancing with the devil. Before I could move forward, I had to confront and heal a lot of shame, anger, hopelessness and guilt. I had to forgive my mother and just as importantly, forgive myself. If I hadn't gone through all of those hard times then, I wouldn't be able to write this book today.

This is the work that must be done. We need to heal

every hurt and understand the web of thoughts, feelings, behaviors, patterns and beliefs that are attached to each one of these wounds so we can heal them once and for all and extinguish and transmute the negative energy that comes along with each wound. All of the old, stored up negative energy has to be released so that you can be free.

I've also found that much of the negative energy that we carry concentrates in different parts of our body. The resulting aches, ailments, and pains are telling us that something needs to be healed within. I believe that the vast majority of the physical pain that we experience at any given time is concentrated, stuck, unreleased negative energy.

As an example, for the past six weeks, as I've worked on editing this book, I've had problems with my left hip, leg, ankle and foot as well pain in my right shoulder. In addition, for some time now, I've experienced painful arthritic changes in my fingers and toes. The left side of our body represents the feminine as the right represents the masculine.

I had been going to a chiropractor and a massage therapist for these ailments for quite a while. My massage therapist Sandra McTeague is a Shaman and is extremely intuitive and awesome. I asked her "What am I not dealing with? The pain is getting better but not going away?" She told me it had something to do with the writing of my book and that something was affecting my stomach.

As she kept working on me, I remembered that as I was working on chapter twelve of this book. I decided to write more openly about family conflict and abuse. It was very uncomfortable for me. I had written about these issues earlier but then deleted what I had written. I realized that I felt that I was being disloyal to my mother and feared hurting her feelings by exposing the part she played in my painful life story. I was sick to my stomach, but I stuck to my decision and kept writing.

As I rewrote that section I was taken back to being 15 years old again and felt the pain of not wanting to expose my mother to the pain of telling her that her husband was raping me. For some reason, I thought it was more important to protect her from pain, than to take care of mine. I didn't understand it then, but I clearly felt that her feelings were more important than mine. I felt like I was telling a dirty family secret that had been kept in the closet so that my mother could continue to live in denial as she had always done.

I understand now that this was another of my faulty belief systems that I needed to heal. I am (we are) not responsible for other's feelings, and I am (we are) just as important as anyone else. We need to accept help as we strive to heal and one of the first steps is to be truthful with our selves and others.

I also now understand that I was living in denial myself by repressing my feelings. The physical pain that I was experiencing was my soul trying to get me to see that I had deep unresolved wounds that needed to be healed as well as forgiveness. My unresolved emotional pain would continue to manifest itself as debilitating physical pain as long as I continued to avoid the inner healing that needed to take place.

We tend to blame and hold others accountable for the same things we are doing ourselves. I was angry that my mother was living in denial but she was simply acting as a mirror image designed to show me my self. I was living in a lot of repressed denial and anger.

At age 15, I told some high school friends about the abuse and the information eventually leaked out to a teacher. Calls were made to my mother and the police, but nothing came of it; I was not believed. So, I exposed my stepfather but that didn't seem to matter to my mother or to the courts. As I told the story to my massage therapist, all of the pain in my body started to release and I felt much better.

Later, as I meditated on this, I was amazed to realize that the old pain of exposing my mother (which, in reality, was exposing my self), created an intense store of energy that manifested itself in the same locations in my body that my mother has always had physical problems with herself. I firmly believe that this goes way beyond genetically inherited physical ailments. I believe that this is our soul manipulating energy to create a level of physical discomfort designed to act as a wakeup call telling us that we have unresolved wounds that need to be healed.

I have also come to understand that some of my physical pain is linked to other faulty beliefs and fears that I had, specifically, that I was an impostor. My fear of shining or being in the limelight is an underlying belief that many of us have that we really don't deserve recognition. My fear of shining was also accompanied by a fear that I would be exposed and ridiculed as a fraud and that my shining meant I was exposing my mother so I could shine and that would be inconsiderate. Both of these fears are faulty and rooted in my childhood experiences. My father would say anything to get by or get what he wanted and I lived in constant fear that his lies would be discovered. I feared that he would be found out to be an imposter. This eventually happened and I was mortified.

Can you see how all of these fears and faulty beliefs are linked together? That is why they are so difficult to separate and heal. You get your mind wrapped around one fear or one belief and you work on that and think you are done with it. But in reality, we find that we are required to keep healing the same basic issues that manifest themselves again at deeper and deeper levels.

It's not unlike the realm of the physical sciences where scientists will tell you that each new revelation, each new understanding about how the universe works only leads to a seemingly infinite series of new questions that need to be addressed and answered. Each door that we open leads us to a whole set of new doors that we need to unlock. This is why we describe our spiritual quest as a process or a journey.

As I mentioned in the prior chapter, some of the negative energy that we have to work on comes from previous incarnations. A great deal of it is also passed down within our family from one generation to the next. We need to rescue these wounded parts of us that were rejected and abandoned by others and by ourselves. The more of this negative energy you transmute, the more treasure is exposed. This is something only you can do; no one can do it for you.

Our wounded selves can be tremendously resistant to the idea of being loved, and it can take a lot of hard work before our wounded inner children can accept our love. I tried giving love to the frightened little wounded children within, but for the longest time, they would not receive it. As I continued to learn how to love myself I was eventually able to understand my innocence, forgive myself, allow love to flow to those self-abandoned parts of me; and now I am able to accept and receive it. This is the process of integration. This is a practice that you will have to do over and over again. It is not one and done. It was a huge epiphany when I realized that I had never understood how to receive or how to give love in a healthy way. It is a miracle to watch and feel the changes as you heal yourself with the help of God.

Many people are afraid to go inside and see what is there. This is normal, however, it is that very fear that keeps us attached to the pain. Even if you feel some fear and ambivalence, it can be of great help to take your guidance with you and ask for peace and contentment. Let your guidance, especially your higher self, role model how to love your little self. Keep pushing through the fears. You are only confronting old memories, the negative energy of past events and experiences.

This work is hard, but necessary. Honor yourself for daring to undertake such a difficult job. It is what you came here to do... awaken from your spiritual unconsciousness, evolve your soul into a state of higher understanding and learn self-love. Many of the things we believe about ourselves, many of the things that are causing us pain and holding us back are irrational and untrue.

Until we overcome these beliefs and feelings we are going to struggle. We can't live lives of self-abandonment and/or denial if we want to be happy and free. Remember, you are not doing this work alone. You have access to God's Kingdom (Universe) within you to love you throughout your journey and shine light on whatever needs to be healed.

You might want to take a few deep breaths right now. Take a piece of paper and write down any fears you have about going inside and starting the journey to healing.

What might you find? What is scaring you the most?

People will often say that they don't remember much about their childhood, or that they had a great childhood. Both of these can be true, but if we look deep enough there are usually events and experiences that we have suppressed/repressed that need to be acknowledged.

Make a timeline marking out your ages in groups of five years. Write down all the positive and negative events that you remember. It won't all come to you at once. You'll probably find that a recollection of one event, whether good or bad, will lead to a memory of other events that you hadn't thought about for years. Work on it for a while until you have remembered and recorded multiple events.

Look at your old school pictures or family photos to see if those images help stimulate memories. Speak with family members and ask them about special or difficult times that they remember when you were young. Your job is to uncover as much as you can. I'm sure that as you continue to work on your timeline, both positive memories and some very negative and uncomfortable ones will come flooding back.

Some of these memories may even come back to you in your dreams. This is normal. You are opening the box where you have hidden and stored all of the painful events and experiences that need to be healed and all of the negative energy that needs to be released.

Journal entry 7/13/15
Working with my 15 year old self with Jesus

15-year-old self: *How vulgar rape is! I don't think anything could feel worse than rape. It is disgusting! I am so broken I can't see, think, or feel. Why would someone hurt me like this? Why, am I bad? What did I do to be treated like this? I hate him and I hate myself! I am suffering and no one cares, no one ever cares about me! How could she let him do this? Tell me why, I don't understand and never will! I feel so alone, ashamed, I am scared; I am angry; I hate him! I never feel safe ever! I always think someone is lurking around and don't trust anything anyone says. I feel dirty.*

Me: *What can I do for you?*

15-year-old self: *Just hold me, keep holding me always, and don't let go of me. I am scared.*

Me: *I am holding you always, just as I am now.*

15-year-old self: *Where is God?*

Me: *He is inside us in our heart.*

15-year-old self: *I can't feel him.*

Me: *I know, but He is here. This is what I want you to do. I want you to breathe and ask God for peace and contentment. (Jesus comes and holds her and blesses her with peace and contentment and soothes her with his love).*

Jesus: *You did a great job you needed to acknowledge her (you). Your 15-year old self is in such fear and pain all of the time. It wasn't long after that you had elbow surgery for Osteomyelitis. You had a lot of physical and emotional pain to deal with.*

Me: *I went through a lot didn't I Jesus?*

Jesus: *Yes you did. It was a lot. Do you see how strong you are to survive all of this pain and be happy now?*

Me: *I do.*

Jesus: *You do not give yourself credit. You have almost always been in pain, until recently. Until you honor all of your pain it is going to keep demanding your attention. The pain you experienced was tremendous. It is time to rest now and honor* *this 15-year old part of you. Comfort her some more, she (you) deserves it and did not get it. Don't be in a hurry. It was the music that you always listened to and smoking pot all the time that kept you from that pain just so you would not feel the depth of despair.*

Me: *(to my 15 year old self) All the nightmares every night, fearful he was coming after you because he said he would. You did not rest and had night terrors constantly, so scared, you had to sleep in our parents room (father and step-mother) and you still didn't feel safe. You just wanted to be held and loved you poor thing. No one understood you had PTSD and self medicated with pot to make it go away. You just wanted someone to love you and make you feel safe.*

15-year-old self: *I don't trust anyone. I don't feel good enough to be loved.*

Me: *I know you feel that way but it is not true, I love you.*

It took a lot for me to face this pain that I repressed many years ago. Until I had the support of my spiritual guides I was afraid to go back and heal the pain by acknowledging and re-feeling these old wounds. Before I had the help of my spiritual guides I didn't even realize that healing was possible. This was just the first of many healing sessions that I had with my 15-year old self.

At first it was as if there was a wall between us. I didn't know how to nurture myself and was apprehensive. I had to repeat the healing process several times as my understanding of self-love grew. Each time, my heart opened wider to her (myself) until I no longer experienced any withholding of love from within myself. I had to come face to face with that part of myself that wanted to die at that age. I am thankful that I never did anything to end my life and instead just numbed myself from the feelings of humiliation and aloneness. Healing is a process and it takes time.

Chapter Seven

THE ILLUSION OF LIFE

We are one consciousness,
one love, one energy for always and forever
What ever you do or feel
resonates throughout the Universe
You must use your power wisely...

As you do this work and slowly draw closer to reuniting with God and coming into alignment with your true purpose in life, the more you'll be able to see everything collectively as one, as the same energy, the same spirit as God. We are not just God's children; we are one with God. Each of us is God and Goddess, masculine and feminine. It is (and we are) all one and the same.

If we all were able to recognize everyone and everything as being the spirit and energy that is God, then there would be peace in the world. I know this sounds idealistic, but this is our soul's purpose, to be a beacon of love and light and have compassion and grace for those who are still unaware and have not yet awoken.

It can be unsettling to discover that much of life is an illusion. We need to realize that, in truth, everything is a reflection of you which encompasses our ego and of God's/Spirit's love and goodness. Much of what you see is a mirror image showing you some part of your self.

One way you could look at this is imagine that you are the author, actor, producer and viewer of a movie, which is the story of your life playing out on a stage in front of you. You have others helping you with supporting roles.

If you are carrying old pain, fear, anxieties, resentments or anger they will be projected onto the stage into this movie and you will continually encounter whatever you are subconsciously suppressing/repressing. If you are the author you get to write a different script. If you are the actor you get to play a different role. If you are the producer of this movie you can chose another perspective. As the viewer you decide if you are satisfied or not. If not talk to the author again, have a consultation with your higher self.

This mirror imaging can create a lot of unnecessary and unwanted drama in your life. It can create painful, negative events as you let these feelings continue to fester within you.

The healing and letting go that you need to do is

absolutely critical in that it will allow you to project and consciously create the life that you want through love, peace, contentment, joy, and passionate purpose, not through fear and pain.

We are all here to work through our grief and misery. We are here to evolve our soul and to learn how to forgive and love. We are also here to create, and your act of creation needs to be in alignment with whatever Gods' calling or life's work is for you. This creation of your new life, a life that is in alignment with your dreams and your true purpose is what you came here to do.

As long as you continue to live life through your ego and unconscious, the life that you are creating will not be in alignment with your divine purpose. That doesn't mean that you can't be successful, happy, or content with some portions or areas of your life. The truth is, you can manifest anything you want, but if what you create isn't in alignment with your higher purpose, your life will lack the passion and joy that you are meant to feel.

We see a lot of tragedy in the world. Too many people are still spiritually asleep and unconsciously creating lives of pain and misery from lessons unlearned. They are suffering and are unconsciously projecting that same suffering and misery energetically/vibrationally onto everyone and everything they encounter.

We can often see this in the workplace where people's negativity creates a hostile environment that results in poor morale that sucks the life and energy out of everyone. Remember, if this describes your work environment, it is mirroring a part of you or showing you something that needs to be healed within you. If you are bringing any of your negative internal energy, or unresolved anger into the workplace environment, you are contributing to the problem. Each coworker is subconsciously doing the same thing. Your energy changes as you do this work and as it changes, it should help to create a more positive dynamic around you.

Don't expect to see a complete change in the environment. You can't make others change their projections and behaviors. But you can change yours by clearing out negative thinking and replacing it with positivity, peace and love. By doing so, you may be able to create positive changes in the way that your co-workers interact with you. It may also be that you have to ultimately remove yourself in order to protect your new energy from a hostile environment.

I spoke before about how energy/vibration wants to harmonize with its surroundings (Barbara De Angeles –'Soul Shifts'). If you think about it, it means that your energy can move in either a positive or a negative direction. It can expand or contract. In a negative environment, it is easy for your newly acquired positive energy to become toxic again. How do we protect our energy? It takes time and practice. In fact, our energy is always expanding and contracting all day long. It is our breath, the pulse of life, and it never stops. I am in the process of learning how to balance my energy and will discuss that whole concept in my next book.

Minimizing your interactions with sources of negative energy is a great strategy, but it's not always realistic. Prayer helps to cleanse our energy. Ask God to clear your energy field and fill you with love, peace and contentment. I imagine a beautiful ring of white light that surrounds and protects me as I go through my day cleansing my energy field and only letting love in or out. Remember, you can link your imagination directly to Spirit if it is motivated by love and comes from your heart. You can also pray to have the other person's energy cleared and ask that they be filled with peace and contentment. I like to say: "peace, love, joy and light abide in me" and then take a deep breath. I learned this simple saying from 'A Course In Miracles.'

I realize that you might be reading this and saying how ridiculous this seems; nevertheless, it works! It isn't easy, but as you become more and more awake, you realize that the illusion of life keeps getting stripped away little by little. You begin to recognize that you can draw on deep reservoirs of loving power within you by accessing your soul or higher self and staying attached to God. Everything around you will begin to appear magical, because it really is.

Journal Entry 10/21/15
Discussion with Jesus

Me: *There has been so much awakening in me the last couple of days it is overwhelming, and trying to put the knowledge into some kind of context has been difficult. I shift from knowing to not understanding and back and forth again.*

Jesus: *I know it feels like discord, but remember that is normal; it is a lot to digest.*

Me: *Please help me to understand.*

Jesus: *I would love to help you understand. I know that in the past you were not ready to hear it yet but today you understand that everything is not as it appears.*

Me: *Yes.*

Jesus: *It is an illusion, but it is very real to you and the people around you. It is God's way of loving you, giving your spirit an experiential exercise. The purpose is to make your soul grow.*

We are all different aged souls and to ultimately understand this is the meaning of life and love.

Me: *But so much of it is tragic.*

Jesus: *Yes, but it is about taking tragedy and growing through it and understanding that through faith, trust, love and perseverance we find meaning to move forward and to give others hope so they can move forward.*

Me: *But we awaken to see that we have not understood the meaning of our past experience. Therefore, we remain stuck in the past with our worries and fears.*

Jesus: *The awakening is to move out of that space into love and purposeful life and meaning.*

Chapter Eight

INHERITED ENERGETIC BELIEF SYSTEMS

Energy is all that life is
It is our job to transform it to love
and that transformation happens only through God...

It's important to remember that everything is working on God's/Universe's timeline, not our own. Everything is already divinely planned. At the right moment, our dreams/desires will unfold. We need to stay in a state of positive belief and expectation always working to be in alignment with God and always believing that whatever we need is on its way, right around the corner. This develops trust and faith that God knows better than we do. We are not doing anything wrong but we are allowing time to control our life. The ticking of the clock creates great pressure.

There is a core belief system that is an integral part of

being human that entails beliefs such as: life is a struggle, I am a victim, I suffer, I am lacking, I will be abandoned, I am rejected, I cannot trust, and I am alone. All of the faulty beliefs come from fear and reside in our unconscious mind when we're impatient and not in alignment with God. None of these faulty beliefs are true.

I learned a great deal by analyzing my personal relationship with my self, other relationships, and my thoughts about what was or was not happening in my life. I began to identify areas in my life where I was constantly struggling. I saw that I always felt a deeply rooted sense of grief, disappointment or judging myself based on whether I was seeing progress in my efforts to manifest whatever I was trying to create at that moment.

If I was working hard to create something but was not seeing the kind of progress that I expected, I immediately felt a deep sense of lack rather than simply accepting that it may not be the right time for that particular desire to be manifested or that everything is in Divine order and I just needed to stay in a state of gratitude.

As I continued to analyze my thoughts, feelings, and reactions to the normal ups and downs of life, I saw how many of my feelings and responses could be traced directly back to this negative core belief system and I came to appreciate how insidious this core pattern of negative beliefs really is.

Just like everything else in the universe, our feelings,

thoughts and beliefs consist of pure energy. This core negative belief system that is part of our basic human nature has a massive energetic impact on us. It operates on every level of our thoughts, feelings and behaviors and, in doing so, has a negative effect on everything that we unconsciously manifest in our lives.

These fears creep in and out of our conscious mind but are always present in our shadow side. This imbedded negative energy has been cultivated in the primitive part of our brain since the beginning of time and becomes food for the ego. The ego uses that energy to create oppression and hostility within us that we then unconsciously manifest in our lives in a variety of ways.

We are all projecting these unconscious beliefs into everything we do and expect. It's ironic that we can create wonderful things out of our heart while at the same time we are unconsciously bringing into our life things that are harmful and destructive. It's the fundamental dichotomy of our human natures. We have a Divine Spirit full of love and an ego full of fears. Our Spirit and our ego will continue to battle one another within us until we finally learn how to recognize our negative belief system and clear out all of the negative energy that comes with it.

Our job then is to learn how to balance and control this negative energy so that we do not react or buy into whatever struggle, lack, suffering, victimization, abandonment, mistrust, rejection etc. that our ego tries to project into our life. Seeing ourselves from a spiritual perspective is seeing that fear and love live side by side within us and realizing that as we continue to do this work, the positive energy of love will overcome the negative energy of our fears and beliefs. Love is the only antidote for fear.

We just need to analyze our thoughts, feelings, and beliefs, stop empowering our negative belief systems, strengthen and nourish the positive energy that comes from our Divine Spirit, and defuse the negative energy of our ego. We lack nothing. We have everything we need. Each and every one of us has come into this world full of abundant possibilities.

Each day, in my meditations, I receive spiritual lessons on how to balance the energy within me. I've come to understand that the relationship we have with ourselves is the most important relationship since it dictates the course and substance of all our relationships with the outside world. Learning self-love and compassion for our feelings and everything about us is key. Learning this lesson and then internalizing it so that it becomes an integral part of my being has been a struggle for me. I suspect it might be for you too because you have to overcome the old belief systems and learn how to explore your own capacity to love your self especially when we are not at our highest at times.

Love and joy are energies just like other feelings and emotions, however, this energy vibrates at a much higher level because it is Divine and it is the only truth.

Many of us want to create abundance, loving relationships, positive careers, etc. and yet we feel like there is something that is blocking our ability to manifest our hopes and dreams. The block is our inherited negative belief system, nothing else. We don't realize the impact that this inherited fireball of fear has on us. It's part of our humanity and has followed us here through all of our previous incarnations, picking up energetic momentum all along the way.

Believe it or not, this negative belief system can serve an immensely useful purpose for us. If we honestly analyze and explore it, we will realize that the ego creates the illusion we call life and, as such, is a huge obstacle that has to be reckoned with. We will see that the ego expresses itself, as oppression, hostility and yes, even love at times. We will also come to understand that whatever we see in the world around us is a manifestation of what exists inside of us.

Therefore, if we want to have a positive effect on the world in which we live, we have to take on the responsibility to fix and heal ourselves from within and to manifest and create love and joy on the outside and make the world a better place.

For example, like most people, I want to create financial affluence in my life but have negative underlying beliefs about being affluent. This isn't at all uncommon.

Those beliefs might be that I have to work hard or struggle to get money, or that people will not like me if I have a lot of money, or maybe I focus on all of the negative things that might happen if I lose my money. These kinds of negative beliefs all come from our inherited belief system that always emphasizes fear, struggle, lack, abandonment, rejection, victimization, etc.

As I drilled deeper in trying to understand this dynamic, I began to recognize patterns of thought that are part of this massive inherited belief system. I grew up seeing my family constantly argue about money. My father's family became estranged over family money and financial matters. There were times as I was growing up, and again as an adult, that financial issues were very real and very painful. In fact, I had declared bankruptcy many years ago. As a result, I developed the energetic belief that wealth and affluence is divisive.

I eventually came to see that those negative energetic beliefs about money and wealth seeped into my first marriage, then into my second marriage, and have also been passed down to my children. What a pity! The negative beliefs regarding money and affluence have been quickly and unerringly passed down through two successive generations in my family.

The real pity is that there is absolutely no truth to it. Money is not divisive; it is the **fear that is divisive.** The fear of lack of money or the fear of lack of anything else (love, etc.) is what becomes divisive. This was a tremendous insight for me because it still comes up on a daily basis in my relationship. It confronts me on a daily basis so that I can slowly but surely learn how to not feed into the old inherited negative belief system.

I will give you an example. Recently I was making reservations for travel. I could spend $200.00 more and have a direct flight versus one that had a 3-hour layover and would get me home later. I deliberated over and over thinking that I should not spend the extra money and I need to make the right choice. I felt a lot of pressure and worry. Do I have the money to spend? Yes, I do but we are trying to stay in a budget. This gets very confusing. I don't believe in lack but I need to stay in a budget, hmmm. Then I thought, my husband would be happier if I took the less expensive flight and I want him to have faith that I want to stay in our budget.

It was interesting that I was having thoughts of suffering and sacrifice if I took the cheaper flight. There is no truth to either of those things. I am neither suffering nor sacrificing. I am making a conscious choice for our budget. First of all, there is no truth to the belief that we have to sacrifice for love, ever. This belief goes way back to a time when people believed they would have to sacrifice to the Gods in order to be loved or show faith. Sacrifice and guilt is just playing the martyr game and seeing your self as a victim. That is a faulty belief that our ego loves to use on us. It fit so neat and tidy into this scenario though, didn't it? Had I not been conscious, I would have missed the lesson and fed into the drama my ego was making for me.

If you think about a negative belief that is a constant problem in your life, and if you look at how you and your family and close friends interact around this belief, you'll see that the people in your life are constantly role-playing (unknowingly) what you need to heal. They are constantly giving you opportunities to drill down into the core of whatever this negative belief may be so that you can understand where it comes from, clearly see how it is negatively affecting you life, and work on clearing it away.

Everything we see happening on the outside of us is simply a mirror reflecting what is going on inside of us. God has given us this amazing mirror so that we can recognize our negative patterns and move forward towards healing and transforming all of this negative energy into light, love and joy.

Money is a common problem, and finding love is another. Perhaps you want to create a truly loving and fulfilling relationship. First, take an honest look at what your core beliefs are about love and your ability to give and receive love. Be honest. Do you believe that loving or being loved is going to be a struggle? Do you fear that you may not find the right person? Are you already projecting the pain that you'd feel if they were to leave you? Are you worrying in advance (even before you've found someone) about whether or not they'd like your children?

If you see these kinds of patterns affecting your hopes and dreams then there's work to be done before you will be able to find the person and create the relationship free and clear of all of your negative beliefs.

I still struggle with this myself as I grow and want to consciously create more in my life. My ego voices still arise at times and whisper fearful, negative things to me about how trying to manifest my dreams will create some sort of struggle, failure, scarcity, rejection, or victimization. I fight to not validate these thoughts or feelings. At times my ego is strong and can very easily take over for a while. At other times I am stronger in my highest and can easily dismiss and disregard them.

Until we learn how to balance and control this negative energy, we are going to keep running into blockages as we try to create or manifest any of our dreams that have previously been associated with our inherited web of negative beliefs.

These books are actually following my progress as I progress along my own personal spiritual journey. To date, I find that the most interesting lesson for me as I try to balance the energy within is learning how to infuse all of that energy with love, light, and joy.

We all need to learn how to manipulate/transform our energy into love, light and joy by balancing it within us. It is an awesome task to be able to balance the energy within us and transform it over and over again to love, light, and joy.

I never had any lessons about how to balance my energy until recently. I received a lesson on the importance of energy balancing from one of my Spiritual Angels. I now understand the purpose of the lesson as a result of listening to my wonderful friend Anayah Joi Holillly on *Angel Heart Radio*, who channeled a beautiful message from Kwan Yin. All we need to offer is love and compassion to ourselves and balance our own energy. When we do so, we affect everything and everyone else.

As I felt sadness, fear and guilt arise in me today I decided to meditate and see where it was coming from. Some of my little wounded children were triggered again by a situation at home. I used the guided imagery to sit with these parts of me and explore what the feelings were. Of course, those feelings were part of the synergistic negative web of misbeliefs and fears.

I recognized that I needed to infuse love and joy into these parts of me by me loving them and telling them that no matter what they are feeling I love them, I will take care of them, and how joyful our life really is. The more I infused love, joy and truth into them (me), the more their internal energy shifted into joy. I did not tell them they were wrong to feel the way they were feeling. I just loved them as they were, and saw the beauty of innocent children who are vulnerable and don't understand the ego. I was creating safety within my self that had nothing to do with anything happening in the world outside.

You have to feel the love and joy within yourself and I do that by connecting to my heart, which is the immediate channel to God. If you just speak the words without feeling the love and joy it does not work. Our job is to transform all of our internal energy to love and joy. We need to be present to stay on top of it and we need to want to take the time to administer self-love.

This takes tremendous patience and practice. God gave us the power to transform and heal all energy with love and joy and the only person we need to do this with is our self. As we do this, it affects everything outside of us without our having to do anything externally but vibrate in our true energy of love and joy. We control our energy (feelings), and as we learn this lesson it affects the universe since we are one collective consciousness of universal energy. Remember, this is a lifetime of work. There is no end date for when a goal is to be met. Positive and negative energy is always flowing and vibrating around us and within us. We will always need to work on balancing these energy flows daily.

As you work on clearing out all of the old pain and relinquishing your negative belief systems, you come into alignment with who you are and who you are meant to be. You will find your true passion and purpose and your creations will be more positive and ever more fruitful.

You don't have to clear away every single bit of negative energy or every fragment of an inherited negative belief system before you start seeing your higher purpose and your creativity. And while it may be sad to recognize how these negative beliefs have affected and harmed past generations of your family, it is a joy to realize that you are the one who is finally breaking those chains and providing freedom for generations of your family yet to come.

Journal entry 3/13/17
with Jesus

Me: *Jesus, please help me understand the synergy of energy. Is synergy the right word or is there a better one? Do the individual fears come together and create the potency of the ego or is it something separate that doesn't have to do with the ego, or does it feed the ego? Is it in us on a cellular level?*

Jesus: *Ok, since you want to know, it is in the core of your being as a human. These are separate feelings or experiences that have followed you through your numerous lives and they pick up an energetic momentum that when they are combined is so much stronger than when they are alone. This energy feeds the immense influence of the ego and inflates it so it is difficult to deal with. It is like gasoline to a car or, better yet, gasoline to a fire.*

Me: *Is it purposeful?*

Jesus: *Yes, it is to the extent that it is how the ego becomes inflated and helps create the illusion. In a sense, yes, it is synergy,* but from a human experience it would be looked upon as negative, but from a Spiritual perspective, it is not. It is all systems go and that is part of what you came here to do, undo and navigate the ego's illusion and its energetic web of blockage, and come back to who you truly are. The energy is so old it is fierce and that is why everyone needs to awaken.

Me: *Am I right about this energy being an undercurrent of negativity and untruths that constantly sabotage the creating and manifesting? There is no blockage other than allowing this energy to resonate within us and believing it.*

Jesus: *Yes, you know it is. You need to have faith in your knowingness.*

Me: *How do we get rid of this matrix of negative energy?*

Jesus: *Just keep doing what you are doing, seeing it, not feeding into it and knowing there is no truth to it. You do not have to suffer or have pain; it is an illusion.*

Me: *I have been getting energy balancing lessons from Angelica (Angel – mama, we all have a mama Angel, I will tell you about them another time). What does all of this have to do with the balancing I am learning?*

Jesus: *You will see, it will all come together shortly.*

Me: *Yesterday, after we had a great discussion and I had this amazing epiphany, I felt great gaining the knowledge and light, and I then went to the computer and was shopping on Amazon for hours just looking for a perfect fun gift for my daughter's wedding, sucked into the abyss of unconsciousness. Why? What happens to the energy within when we go up, why do we crash into unconsciousness after?*

Jesus: *You don't have to but it is a normal and common reaction.*

Me: *Why does more light expose more darkness or illuminate it and then we get sucked into it and go unconscious?*

Jesus: *You are awesome and so persistent. You don't give up do you? I love that about you. It exposes more darkness when you are in the light but you have not learned yet how to balance the energy after the light. That is what you are working on, to keep your energy in balance through both light and darkness. Do you feel exhausted now since you had another epiphany about dark and light energy?*

Me: *Yes.*

Jesus: *Do you see what I mean? This takes time to balance. Most people do not recognize this is even happening in them.*

Me: *What can I do so I don't go unconscious again?*

Jesus: *Take a few minutes to breathe, eat lunch and look at nature in your backyard. In the past, you drove yourself to the point of exhaustion. Even then, you would make yourself do more or run errands, etc. Now it is okay for you to just relax.*

Chapter Nine

FEEL THE POWER

You are the master of your internal world
It is up to you to rise up and assume responsibility
Take on the challenge of separating from your ego
You have all the spiritual guidance within you to lead you
You are the only one that can make this happen
No one can do this for you...

We all want power over our external world. You are now learning that you have that power, but your power to create a positive life can only come from a loving, open heart, not through fear or the manipulation of people, places and things. Love unlocks the door to everything you wish your life to be. Instead of speaking judgment, criticism, negativity or lack, we should speak love, healing, blessings and abundance for our selves and everyone else. You have the power to bless yourself and others.

We discussed before that we are one with God and that by blessing our selves and others we are shifting our lives and the lives of others in very positive directions. Try practicing this. Give it a couple of months and see the changes that you create.

Sometimes you see the change immediately. You will also see that if you start projecting negative thoughts about yourself and others you will create negativity and bring it back upon yourself. It takes practice to have a conscious awareness of what is happening in your mind with your thought patterns, behaviors and feelings.

Your goal is to get all of the old patterns disassembled so their energy dissipates. When you notice a negative pattern, take deep breaths. Breathe into your heart and bring yourself back into a place of peace. It takes a long time to acquire the ability to consistently see and not react to all of our patterns; it is a journey. It's a difficult skill to develop since we are still constantly dealing with our ego and the realities of day-to-day life.

Ego can also trick us into thinking we are in our highest when we aren't, and that we have an open heart when we don't. Over time, you will learn how to tell the difference. You keep climbing the stairs, up and down, until you find yourself just going up.

You need to acquire and master a lot of skills just to get to this point. Your spiritual guidance will help you acquire and enhance the skills you need. Each day, I ask my guidance what I need to do, what I need to focus on, and what they want to share with me…in essence, what is your will for me today.

I am always told that my guidance wants me to be happy and that I am loved. This is my guidance's daily message because it realizes that happiness is constantly eluding us due to our ego. It is a reminder to check in with yourself about your happiness and if you are not happy, why not? I have often thought to myself how can I have so much love within me, so much constant validation, and still not be happy; it just doesn't make sense. The simple answer is that I am human, and if I am unhappy, it is because my ego is in control. We constantly have to shift ourselves back into a state of happiness, joy and gratitude.

If you are attentive and quiet, you will hear constant Spiritual feedback and direction throughout the day. As time goes on, you will hear that feedback more clearly. Trust your guidance. It will never steer you wrong. Even if you are hesitant, follow your guidance and see what happens. You will come to see that your guidance knows what is best for you even more that you do, because you have probably been living unconsciously with your ego in charge with all of its negative and delusional thinking.

Your guidance is leading you to your highest which will align your will with God. Work on trusting your guidance. Right now, you may not be able to clearly see your life's purpose or calling that your soul and God agreed upon. It may not turn out to be what you think it is. Your purpose and the expression of that purpose may be much different (whether greater or smaller) than you could ever imagine. Either way, it still has the same value.

When you are ready, your guidance will start to prepare you. All of us are impatient and want to know what God is calling us to do and be. This is especially true if we are older because we feel that we have wasted so much time. You haven't wasted time. You are exactly where you should be in the story of how your life is to unfold. One of my lessons is understanding that all I have to do is be happy, be myself, and be excited about the life in front of me, and then everything comes in due time. This sounds simple; it's not. I have had to dismantle my belief systems and let go. It is still a work in progress, however, I've been rewarded all along the way.

We are learning to slow down and not allow self-imposed time limits and goals to dominate our lives. Ego will berate you for not mastering a certain skill yet, even your spiritual awakening! It will keep pushing and prodding you, but all it is really doing is creating stress and taking you out of your highest. None of what the ego says is true. This work takes patience, practice, and the ability to integrate all of our newly acquired knowledge into our daily lives without fighting it out with our ego.

Break the chains of your inherited programing by being loving to yourself. Do the work that needs to be done. It is as though you are just starting to understand how to play the piano. You can't expect to become a concert pianist overnight. It takes long, hard work. You can't force it to happen quickly. Don't listen to your ego and expend energy when you hear ego judging you. Ignore it and be aware that it may not stop; it is what it is. Every day I say lots of prayers. Here are some of my favorites.

I am a blessing, I am blessed
God, please bestow the blessings you have blessed
upon me to _____ (fill in the blank) heal me and
heal _____(fill in the blank).

I also love the Ho'oponopono Prayer, which is an ancient Hawaiian practice of reconciliation and forgiveness (Wikipedia definition). You can use this prayer when you feel that anything is going wrong in your life. If you feel that someone has wronged you, or if you are thinking negative thoughts about someone, or about yourself, you end up carrying the pain or judgment. This prayer helps you shift perspective. You can say this prayer silently to yourself or out loud. In reality this prayer helps you clear negative energy. In essence you are forgiving yourself for what you have created and thanking the person or situation for showing you your creation, regardless of whether it was created consciously or unconsciously.

Please forgive me
I'm so sorry
I love you
Thank you

Chapter Ten

LET IT BE

Be honest and true to yourself
This is how you become a blessing to others...

It is important to accept where we are and what is happening in our lives. When we resist, we are unnecessarily expending emotional energy. We waste so much energy day in and day out that it dims our light within. As we have seen, that energy could be put to far more useful and creative purposes. Resistance causes stress and creates a toxic environment, physically, emotionally and spiritually. We don't want to resist the ego. We need to lovingly accept that it is there. We do not need to listen and follow its message. Instead we want to tune into our higher self for guidance.

Now think about what experiences in your life you have been resisting or not accepting since the time of your earliest memories. Everyone has experienced some kind of trauma, whether large or small. We all define trauma differently. One person's major trauma may seem relatively insignificant to another. Many of us struggle with past traumas that have left us feeling hurt, flawed, depressed, anxious, unloved, abandoned, rejected, and alone. We don't know how to let go of past pain. Our ego lives in that world of past pain with all of our old wounds. Our unhealed inner wounded children live in the feeling that we need to constantly worry and strategize how to protect ourselves from any kind of pain or suffering. We get stuck in survival mode. Your ego thinks it knows what will keep you safe, but it's all irrational and untrue and keeps you living in fear.

We can't heal if we wallow in the past and the programing associated with it. We just keep projecting the pain into our life. We resist letting go and feel justified in blaming our selves and others for past pain and trauma. Our inability to let go of the past keeps us from being present. Why do we resist letting go? Why don't we just accept what is or what was?

We resist because we don't want to take responsibility for our feelings, and don't know how to process our pain. We don't see how these past negative experiences fit into our bigger picture. Remember, before we were born we picked our life's path. We chose the people and experiences that we would encounter. When we chose this path we didn't understand pain and misery. As a soul we didn't experience these things. But the soul's goal is to evolve its consciousness to a higher level and, unfortunately, much of the time that evolution comes from witnessing suffering and misery.

If you never experienced any trauma or suffering you might not be reading this book right now. You wouldn't be trying to learn how to evolve and transcend the suffering, how to align yourself with God, how to find your gifts and express them in a way that is in accord with your true purpose. However, I do believe that we all carry the inherited energy of all of our past grief and suffering regardless of what we are experiencing in this life.

My early years were filled with pain. I experienced a lot of trauma from emotional, physical, and sexual abuse. I spent much of my life being angry and building an invisible shield of protective armor (my ego) so that I could avoid pain in the present and future but I was resisting what needed to be healed from the past. In reality, that armor (putting a cement wall around my heart) caused more pain. I never recognized that my armor was the cause of the pain I was experiencing until I started to do this work.

My armor stopped the flow of love coming in and out of my heart. Even though I felt so much love in my heart for my children and others, they never got to feel the depth of that love. Instead, what they experienced was all of my fears and my negative programing projected onto them. They received only the smallest sliver of the love I felt for them.

I will give you an example of resistance from my own life. As I discussed earlier in Chapters six and twelve, at age 15, I was molested and raped several times by my step-father and I had trouble processing the trauma of why it happened and all the feelings I had from this violent experience. When I eventually revealed what had happened not everyone believed me. I buried all of my fears, anger, hate and just tried to move forward, to go on and put it behind me.

Over the years I worked on some of the anger and feelings of betrayal but I really didn't understand at the time that I was only digging into them on a superficial level. I wasn't able to totally accept my pain, empty myself of all of it through self-love, and forgive myself and the other persons involved until I started doing this spiritual work. Initially, I had to forgive myself for not undertaking the work of healing sooner than I did. But I realized that this was simply due to my mistaken belief that I couldn't handle the pain and the belief that I was justified in my anger and blame. It affected my whole life.

I eventually came to see that at different stages in my life I expressed a lot of repressed self-hatred and withheld love from myself and from those around me. As my children reached those same ages, I unknowingly projected all of that negative energy onto them. When you have experienced sexual abuse it is common to re-experience the feelings associated with that trauma when your children become the same age as you were when the abuse occurred.

It manifested itself primarily as me being fearful and trying to control everything in an effort to protect them from being hurt by anyone. This is how the projection works. I passed on to them all that I had not healed in myself. If you've ever parented young teenagers, you can imagine how that turned out. They reacted accordingly.

This happened because I was living unconsciously and not in contact with what was truly going on inside me or outside of me. My children were safe. As we all have, I had inherited generations of emotional baggage and negative energy and programing that had been passed on to me. My children were not just getting my baggage and programing, they were getting the whole multi-generational package. I also know I passed on many wonderful attributes to my children as well. It all gets mixed into the pot of who we are. It's all part of the fabric of our humanity. We are all recipients and, in turn, we all become givers; it's generationally transmitted.

Maybe you see your children on a wrong path...acting out and behaving in ways that trigger all your fears and angers. Maybe it's because you haven't yet dealt with your own traumas, belief systems and pain.

They are a reflection of what you keep hidden from yourself. They are your mirrors. Your children will receive your energy and will act it out in their own lives and within their own families unless we (and they) do the work of recognizing what needs to be healed within and letting go. If you are able to recognize, acknowledge and heal all of your feelings and pain, your children benefit. If you can change your energy to love, openness, and acceptance, you can help change their energy in the same way. There is no greater gift you could give them.

Chapter Eleven

LET IT GO

There once was a young prince in Egypt,
Who loved to play outside in the sun
His heart filled with joy just from
taking in the radiance of light and feeling loved.
He believed that this light was the source of
everything that was good and alive.
He nourished himself in this light everyday, as
much as he could knowing that someday he would
not have this opportunity.
He believed there would come a day that he would
no longer see the sun. He didn't realize that the sun
and its radiance is connected to something so much
bigger and that the radiance was actually within him.
Upon his death he recognized that all of that light
and love was already within him, that the sun was
just a reflection of him, his life force.

We need to let go of everything. We need to release the negative programing, the pain, the belief systems, the blame...whatever is holding us back. All of these things become attached to us, just like our arms or legs, but we need to let them go. Evolving your soul isn't easy. It isn't easy getting to the necessary level of acceptance and acquiring the ability to honor others for the role they played in your life. They played their part in your story and did their best to help your soul evolve, just as you played your part in their story/life. Getting to a place of forgiveness, acceptance, and letting go takes time; but once you get there, you are free.

Your ego's sole purpose is to try to get love from others and to avoid pain. It has been trying to understand the purpose of the misery you have suffered, but it can never do so, and it never wants to let go. It is impossible for your ego to ever have any true understanding. It is irrational, does not understand truth, does not accept blame/responsibility, and does not believe in anything spiritual. This is why our ego is the source of so much of our resistance to spiritual awakening and growth.

Ego makes us feel justified in holding on to our illusion. It makes us feel a certain righteous indignation for the pains we have suffered and we think that that righteous indignation gives us power or leverage over other people and/or situations in our life. As far as your ego is concerned, all of the misery you have suffered cannot be any of your doing so it blames others. The ego is very judgmental towards us as well. It simply does not understand God's higher truth.

As you continue to grow spiritually, you'll be able to understand the purpose of your past suffering. It was purposeful and was a necessary catalyst to help you to learn your soul's lessons. However, there is no need to keep hanging onto the suffering like your favorite pair of jeans that you can't throw away. We need to create space inside of our selves by letting go.

This space allows all the talent, creativity and purpose within you to emerge. Everyone who played a role in helping you learn those lessons should be celebrated, even those who were the cause of so much of the pain and suffering. Those people were simply playing the part you assigned to them.

As your soul grows, it becomes easier to see everyone in your life as a miracle and a blessing, and to understand that you are a blessing in their lives as well. You may not see it, but you are helping others to learn their lessons. When we transcend, the love and light we project helps take others to a higher level of understanding. We are all students. We are all teachers.

Moving beyond all the misery allows you to live from your heart and create a safe and loving vibration for yourself. It also encourages others to be in harmony with you and to grow within themselves. When you discover your gifts, you will bring enlightenment and love to others, no matter how your gifts and talents are expressed. The expression of your gifts will come from your soul and your soul speaks to other souls.

Since we are all on different paths and are at different levels of consciousness, the expression of our gifts will be geared to multiple levels of understanding, interests and peoples' unique Spiritual curriculum. Your guidance will help you understand this. No gift, or expression of a gift, is more important than another.

One of the most difficult challenges we face as we practice letting go of our pain and misery is gaining the ability to see everyone we encounter (including yourself) as special to God and a miracle from God. Contrary to what our ego tells us, no one is better than any one else. No one rates higher than another. It is only our ego that needs to place everyone in a hierarchy of importance. This comes from our smallness, not from our highest. God loves and values you just as much as me. Each of us needs to love and value others as much as we love and value ourselves. Yet feeling this way about our selves, from a healthy perspective not a narcissistic one (ego) takes time.

This is where we get caught up in so many relationship struggles. You can only love someone else as much or as well as you love your self. Our ego will often pretend to show love and honor for others in an effort to gain love and acceptance for itself because it believes we need attachments. When we transcend and can love our selves fully, we can then love others fully without attachment or expectation. We can accept and honor their humanity and our own. This is what sets us free from the chains of living in fear and isolation.

Journal Entry 2/5/16
With Jesus during an extremely windy day

Jesus: *I always have your hands, if you drift too far away, I will always gently pull you back in. I will keep you safe.*

Me: *I give Jesus a hug, I feel needy for that hug.*

Jesus: *It does not matter; this is where you come for those hugs.*

Me: *(Jesus fills me with his love, makes me feel safe, no one else can do that, I feel very loved).*

Jesus: *I will always hold you, even if you cannot see, feel or* *hear me. I have my arms wrapped around you and carry you in my heart.*

Me: *You are so beautiful and I am so grateful. I want to do that for others.*

Jesus: *You cannot rescue people Debbie. They have to want to follow your light; you cannot make them see. I know you worry about others.*
Me: *Yes I do. People can be so negative and constricted and yet be so positive and beautiful.*

Jesus: *Yes, you are seeing yourself, and yes you see their spirit through their ego.*

Me: *The ego can be so ugly.*

Jesus: *Yes, but it serves a purpose; it is the protector.*

Me: *But it takes over and it is not needed.*

Jesus: *Yes, it is part of your soul's journey to understand you are human and your ego will always be with you. It is your job to not listen to it. Your spirit is in charge of you.*

Me: *It feels like a war.*

Jesus: *Yes, it is a battle for a while. We cannot be passive with it; your ego will just take advantage.*

Me: *How do I build my strength in this area?*

Jesus: *Take better care of yourself; do yoga today. You need to dance more and take walks, eat better and stop staying up so late. Ask me to help you. I want you to be in step with me. Everything comes together when you are ready. You are impatient and want to do everything now rather than in its own time. We cannot force things. I see you noticed the wind in the palm trees. Even though it bends and the leaves are being blown everywhere, the trunk still stays steady and rooted to come up straight. This is you. No matter what goes on, you still come back. Stand up straight to let your roots take hold so nothing can unearth you. You are already rooted but have little awareness to how strong those roots are. They are immensely strong. Remember, God has told you that you are a rock of strength. You just need to see it and use it appropriately when needed. Your ego keeps bending the branches but you always have a strong trunk and pop back up. The work you are doing is very difficult; do not minimize it. Everyone chooses jobs or things they want or don't want to do and many will choose not to do this work.*

Me: *(This is my mind, it jumps all over the place). I was looking at the mess in the refrigerator trying to clean it before* *we moved and it was overwhelming. Old stuff stuck on the shelving, things not thrown away, it was all clutter. I guess it is like my mind. Old pain stuck to things, leaking onto other parts, making it messy and ugly, just like what happens in my head.*

Jesus: *That is a good analogy.*

Me: *It is overwhelming to clean up, just like cleaning up my mind. It's easier to be passive and let it keep leaking and affecting other parts of my life than to clean it and fix it. Being passive isn't a good strategy. The mess becomes more sticky and harder to clean up; it affects everything. I need to stop revolting against my self and stop being passive with me.*

Jesus: *Stay focused on me and don't let anything shake you that goes on around you. Stay steady with me even if you have to hold on tighter, I will never let go. There is no storm within me. When you are with me there will only be peace and calm.*

Chapter Twelve

FORGIVE, FORGIVE, FORGIVE

Our journey is about growing our heart
It is the only thing that matters
Forgiveness is the path...

It was October 2014, only 2 months into my awakening, that I had a very strange Spiritual interaction with my deceased stepfather who had raped me when I was younger. I had a long drive to the airport to be with my mom who was going to have back surgery. I had been in a state of joy and felt cared for by my Spiritual guides, and as I drove we chatted about life.

Subtly, another voice came through and I heard, "Debbie, I want to apologize to you for what I did. I am very sorry, I should have never done anything like that to you. Please forgive me. You are a wonderful person and you did not deserve to be treated like that. Please forgive me." I was horrified! I knew it was my stepfather's voice. All I could think about was how did he have the ability to contact me. I didn't want to hear his voice, even if it were for the apology I always wanted. I was very upset and confused and told him, "I will think about it" and I shut it down. I did not want to talk with him.

As I continued driving I started to talk with God about it and I was given room to pause so I could process what had just happened. I was upset that anyone could come through on a Spiritual channel, especially if I didn't want them to. God knows exactly what He is doing. Your guides are wonderful at knowing when you need time to sift through and process your feelings.

I realized that it was time for me to forgive and let go. I had been blaming my stepfather and others for everything that went wrong in my life. I finally recognized that I needed to take responsibility for the last forty-two years of my life and that it was now time for me to heal, forgive and let go. The abuse happened when I was fifteen, but I am the one who held on to the pain and carried it forward with me.

I asked God to help me forgive. I told God everything that occurred and how I felt about it and how it affected my life in detail. I then asked for forgiveness for not letting go and allowing the pain to affect every area of my life, which, in turn, affected others. He told me I was forgiven, that I do not have to carry the burden anymore and that I did not have awareness of what I was doing by not letting go. I accepted my stepfather's soul's apology, forgave and let go.

This then gave me the opportunity to look at my parents and many others for whom I had been holding hostility, blame, unconscious anger, and thereby withholding love from them. It was my ego's way of punishing them, yet I was only hurting myself. I did not understand the depth of my feelings towards everyone because the feelings hid in my unconscious. I kept them suppressed because I did not want to deal with them, after all I liked my happy little life. I went through the same process with God again seeking to forgive each person and my self. It was very freeing.

I actually had to do some deeper work with my mother and God. I had caused her a tremendous amount of pain by not speaking to her for fourteen years (from ages 22-36) due to the rape and my feelings that she was an abusive bystander. She did not believe what happened and supported my stepfather when we went to court. She was stuck in denial and blamed my biological father for creating a hoax. She acted as if nothing had happened.

The pain that I had been feeling as a result of her actions was overwhelming, and I felt it was easier to cut her out of my life than to go on pretending that nothing had happened and everything was okay. One day, after fourteen years of not speaking with my mother, some- thing inside of me shifted and, without knowing exactly why, I no longer felt it was right to not have a relationship with my mother anymore. I recognized that I was the one who was withholding love from my self and abandoning me. What I wanted from my mother was something I was not giving to my self. This was not her fault, she was not able to give it to herself and therefore, was not able to extend it to me. She was my mirror.

I am the only one responsible for me, nobody else is. It was easier to blame my mother than to take responsibility for my own feelings. I didn't know how to take respon- sibility, I was never taught that. Everyone in my family overtly and covertly blamed everyone else for their unhap- piness. What I witnessed at home as a coping mechanism for this was the silent treatment, abuse, rejection, talking about others and lack of forgiveness. There were no open conversations about feelings, you weren't supposed to have them.

God taught me how to take responsibility through love. I was not 15 years old anymore I was 57. Victimization, rejection and abandonment were some of the karmic lessons I had to work through and my mother was an enormous teacher.

Wow, this drive to the airport brought up so much for me. The impetus of my Spiritual awakening stemmed from a family conflict that I had with my son and his wife.

I felt that they were withdrawing from our relationship. I thought, how terrible it would be to not have them or my grandchildren in my life. That would break my heart.

I realized that this was the very thing I had done to my mother for fourteen years, and it struck me like lightening. My heart was filled with sadness and grief. I cannot imagine the pain my rejection must have caused her. Although some might say I was justified, at that moment, I realized I had not forgiven her and that I punished her by not talking to her and keeping her from her grandchildren until they were seven and nine years old. Yet, even though I reached out to reestablish my relationship with my mother, I didn't truly or completely forgive her. I was guarded and standoffish and continued to withhold love. I did not know how to let go on the one hand and still keep myself emotionally safe on the other.

My fear was really just an illusion. The truth is, our soul, our spirit is always safe; it can never be harmed, especially if you look at life as just a dream. However, we create emotional safety within our self. No one else can do this for us. I had to learn how to create safety within me that no one can take away. This is established by deepening your relationship with God and understanding that you are truly safe. This is one of the lessons that my soul needed to learn before it could mature and evolve to an even higher state of consciousness.

As I kept driving I thought, how could I have been

so cruel? It doesn't matter what she did. I never want to be cruel to anyone, especially someone I love. I had built so many walls around myself I didn't realize the effect it had on other people. Each and every day, I was fighting demons that existed only in my mind, put there by my ego. That day, as I drove to the airport in my car, the process of true forgiveness and healing began.

Even though the healing process has begun, it still takes time. Complete healing doesn't always come instantaneously. Not long ago when I was speaking with my massage therapist who is also a Shaman, I recognized that I was still not seeing my mother as innocent, valued, and vulnerable. What I had failed to understand again is that we are each projecting our own self onto others. I was not yet seeing myself as innocent, valued or vulnerable, and I kept projecting that onto my mom and others.

It took some time to come to terms with this. Slowly and surely, as I came to accept the fact of my own innocence and that I was not shameful or guilty, I was able to see my mother in the same light. She was doing the best she could, the best she knew how to do. The truth is that, without knowing or realizing it, I was the creator of this painful story. It was quite a shock to realize how powerful our projections can be. My relationship with my mother is still a work in progress, but thanks to the forgiveness and healing that has occurred so far, I feel much better about where things stand in our relationship today. Which is a mirror image of how things stand within my relationship with my self. Everything is about us.

This healing also helped me to see one of my most harmful illusions, that there is a lack of love for me. This negative feeling that I lack love is an example of the inherited energetic belief patterns that I described in chapter five. It was a huge breakthrough for me to finally be able to see that my mother actually does love me fully, as she can. It was an equally important breakthrough for me to be able to accept the way she expresses her love even though it was not necessarily the way I wanted or needed to experience it. This can only happen with complete forgiveness. The next step is recognizing that I am the only one who needs to love, to be love. The love of my self and the act of self-love is the only necessary love.

On a deeper level, what I was seeing was my own lack of love for my self. I was withholding love from my self and then withholding it from others. I believed and therefore projected that I was not enough, and that others could not love me. Ultimately, what I was projecting was my belief that God didn't fully love me as I was...He may love others, but not me.

I am the only one who needs to love me and that is enough because God's love is enough.

The truth is that I know that everyone is a part of me and every relationship we have is a reflection of our relationship with our self, which reflects our relationship with God. This includes how we relate to everything on this earth.

Many years ago someone read my astrological chart. I don't remember much of what I was told, but I do remember that he told me that one of my flaws was that: "You cannot hold onto love." This haunted me. Today, I understand that there is no truth to this. I suspect that it is one of those negative energy belief patters that can get passed from one generation to the next or from one incarnation to the next. The truth is, love lives inside of me, not outside of me.

The depth of pain between mother and daughter for many of us is heartbreaking. If we don't forgive our own mothers and heal our own pain, we will unwittingly pass it along to our own daughters.

If you need to forgive and heal the relationship with your mother or with anyone else, you need to see that person's soul, not their ego. They are innocent. I had to apply this lesson not just in my work with my mother but with all of the other people I needed to forgive. As I traveled along on my journey I also learned that the negative experiences I had were part of the lessons my soul needed to learn, that I had picked my parents to help teach me these lessons, and I needed to honor everyone's role in helping my soul mature and grow in its consciousness. Jesus taught me that all of the hurts we receive and the pain we feel are actually just part of a dream anyway, that it never really happened even though it seems completely real to us as we experience it.

Your Soul does not hurt you, your ego does. This is why doing this work is so important. We need to have self-discipline and understand that this dichotomy is within us and that we are the only ones that can control the ego and wake up from the illusion that it creates.

My father passed away in 2008. Over the past two years, I've had the opportunity to spend a lot of time with my father working on forgiveness and healing. During a meditation, God created a special beach island where my father was sitting by the water. God chaperoned me as we swam to the beach. I took my little wounded four-year old self with us. God brought me to my father and told me that I needed to discuss with him all the hurts we were holding onto due to his emotional and physical abuse as I was growing up. God went back to the water and just waited. We shared forgiveness, apologies and love, and I felt a tremendous sense of relief within me. It was a beautiful and healing experience. Forgiveness is the doorway to our heart and freedom.

There are always two sides to forgiveness, the side of the one forgiving, and the side of the one being forgiven. When we forgive, we also need to take responsibility for the impact of how our passing judgment and holding on to our hostility has affected both our self and the other party.

All of the things I didn't heal within myself, either

because I was stubborn and thought I was right or because I simply wouldn't let anyone help me, affected my relationship with my children and our family. Unfortunately, it also affected my children's relationships with others as well. The inability to let go and forgive is toxic to everyone and everything.

Yet, as all of this poison is being spread around we can't see it because of our ego's overwhelming need to be right, to be holier than thou, and to be justified. This then is the inevitable outcome when we self abandon and allow the ego to take control.

We need to forgive our selves and others for not being perfect. The lack of forgiveness is poison to our soul. Forgiveness melts our heart and expands it. Holding a grudge suffocates our heart and contracts it. When our heart contracts everyone around us is negatively affected, especially the people we love, most of all, ourselves.

When we turn away from forgiveness we inevitably seek validation or revenge, and neither works. There's no real justification for failing to forgive. Failing to forgive changes nothing. Forgiveness and healing change everything. While forgiveness can't take us back in time and undo whatever event caused our hurt and pain, it can release us from our pain and once and for all stop the spread of poison in our life and in the lives of those we love. I still have to forgive myself daily for thoughts my ego brings to me. It is never ending because I am still working on not judging my ego. I am learning that it is all in Divine order, our ego is not a mistake within our humanity. Our ego is not a flaw, it is Divine perfection.

I just wanted to mention the role of trauma in our lives. Each person individually decides whether something they experienced was traumatic to them. How something affects one person is not always the same way it affects another. The symptoms that develop from trauma may create an unwillingness to revisit and process the events, feel the feelings, and acknowledge what happened. This is what is referred to as Post Traumatic Stress Disorder.

These symptoms stop anything that encourages us to examine those feelings. In fact, avoidance of dealing with anything having to do with the trauma is the common coping mechanism of the victim. This in itself creates more symptomology and therefore, healing seldom if ever occurs. Typically, people stay in a state of fear, anxiety, and depression or their symptoms are repressed by self-abandonment. This is all the work of our ego. It believes we can't manage our feelings and tries to protect us.

Unfortunately, the ego's method of protecting us is to constantly tell us that we are unsafe and to replay the trauma event in our mind over and over and over again. We are the only ones who can rescue those hurt parts of us. No one else can do it for us. Trauma is very treatable if we can get past the lies and deceptions of our ego and let the miracle of forgiveness and healing begin.

Chapter Thirteen

PERFECTION IN HUMANITY

In the stillness of a quiet mind
you see the dynamic of the Ego and your Highest
It is pure Spiritual perfection...

We look upon our humanity and believe that we are broken and imperfect as a result of our experiences and our inherited programing. As a soul, we are already perfect; we are not broken. In truth, the combination of Soul and human is Divinely ordered and is perfect. This doesn't mean that we shouldn't continue to try to evolve our soul.

Our ego looks at our life's experiences and believes that we're broken and need to be fixed. Our ego blames others for the brokenness that it thinks it sees. With our ego in charge, we then try to fix others because we see them as broken. This is called codependent behaviors. In truth, when we see what we think is the brokenness of others we are really only seeing a reflection of ourselves and the belief that we are broken.

We don't need to be fixed. We need to be healed from the belief that we are broken and flawed in the first place, or that others are broken as well. We need to accept our feelings and be compassionate and loving towards them in order to heal them and give others the space to do the same. We really can't truly understand other peoples' journeys or what they must go through or the lessons that need to be learned.

Just because we may feel hurt, sadness, or anger doesn't mean we are broken, it means we are human; were supposed to have feelings. What we need to do is to stop reacting to the negative feelings that are inflated by our ego. It takes time to understand the difference between having a part of you that is in pain versus your ego exacerbating negativity or fear within you. When we take responsibility to heal our wounds with love and compassion then we can release and let go of them.

Can we see our selves and others as being on a Spiritual journey? We have a life to experience and lessons to learn. Some people make tragic or self-defeating choices. When we encounter one of these individuals we have to remember that she/he is also role modeling for us to help us heal something that we need to heal, or to help us understand an important life lesson.

They are role modeling for us, but they are also working on their own journey and there is nothing wrong with where they are in that process, even if they are strung out on drugs. We are not to judge because we do not understand everything. This is very challenging for us because we view everything and everyone through the lens of our social and inherited programming that we believe something is wrong with the other person's journey and there is no truth to this.

This doesn't mean that we shouldn't reach out to help others when appropriate. As long as the other person wants help, then we can have a positive impact by loving and accepting them. If they do not want help, then we need to learn to stay in a space of compassion and love for them and experience (feel) the grief, sadness, and frustration we feel. We cannot fix or rescue anyone. We can only fix and rescue ourselves. If others reach out to us for help we can point them in the direction of healing, but we can't heal them ourselves, only God heals hearts and the person has to be open to it.

We can never know what someone else's Spiritual curriculum is or the details of what their journey is all about. This is the complexity of what is actually occurring as we witness the suffering of others and want to help save and rescue them. The lesson is that only God heals us, we cannot heal others. Only God can mature the soul.

This is a difficult concept but I am going to try to

explain it as best I can based on a thought that came to me recently during a meditation.

As humans, we tend to attach labels to everything we encounter. We label things as good or bad, negative or positive, pretty or ugly and so on. We even label different parts of ourselves. We attach labels to our body image, our thoughts, feelings, our perceived skill sets, our behaviors, careers, etc. This labeling leads to a kind of internal separation, such as: this part of me is good or this part is bad, this is acceptable and this is not. It's almost as though you are seeing your self in a prism where each facet is reflecting a separate part of you that you have labeled good or bad.

As a therapist I had to diagnose clients. Many of my clients fell into a clinical diagnostic category known as Borderline Personality Disorder (BPD), which simply means that you have a defective personality due to lacking the ability to emotionally regulate and over-reacting to perceived abandonment, rejection and fears. This disorder starts around 2 years old and stems from abuse or neglect, especially emotional neglect when parents are emotionally unavailable to a child.

I believe that what is clinically labeled Borderline Personality Disorder is the result of the internal and external separation that occurs when we attach a label or value judgment to each and every part of us. I've come to believe that no one is broken or defective; there is no truth to this or any other diagnosis. Everything that we experience is happening for a reason whether we understand it or not. No one is broken or flawed. We humans are immensely complex creatures and it is the ego that believes something is wrong with us.

Like a prism, we have innumerable facets. The more we label each facet, the harder it is to form a cohesive, well-functioning personality. I believe that a person that we clinically diagnose as having BPD is someone who is struggling with an immature emotionally neglected frightened ego that is scared with no coping skills and is trying to avoid suffering, just like everyone else. This is the crux of all behavior is trying to get love or avoiding pain.

We all exhibit traits of BPD in varying degrees because each of us has an ego that creates feelings of separation. The more spiritually evolved our soul may be, the less our ego is in control and the fewer "clinical symptoms" we'll exhibit. As a result, I no longer believe in assigning traditional clinical diagnoses to people and that was one of the reasons why I decided to stop practicing traditional therapy. I now understand that clinical "symptoms" are a normal part of each person's spiritual journey.

What I have learned is that it is the energetic experiences that we have in early childhood that actually create neural pathways in the brain and also change gene expressions. I will talk more about Epigenetics and Neural

Plasticity in a future volume. Again, it is the exchange and molding of energy that creates all of the things we like to call flaws.

We have tolerance for certain facets and not for others based upon what our ego tells us, as well as on what we have 'learned' from our programing. Our job is to stop assigning labels to these facets and accept the prism as a whole. That whole piece of glass is perfect with everything in it, no matter what it is. All facets in the prism combine to make the whole, and this is the perfection. The prism contains light and darkness, since it plays a role in our evolution and is divinely ordered. There is nothing wrong with anyone.

For myself, my prism facets would include my soul, my higher self, a sad part of me, a happy side, a vulnerable side, a fiery side, a responsible side, a very focused side, an unfocused side, an irresponsible side, a funny side, a serious side, an independent side, a dependent side, my ego, my shadow side, etc.

Most of us are looking for perfection or only seeing ourselves worthy if the whole prism is reflecting only good or positive things that our society tells us are acceptable. We've practiced the art of only showing our 'acceptable' traits to the world and have tried to hide the other parts because we deem them negative.

All the stress and anxiety within us comes from this feeling of being on a stage where we can only show certain traits and have to hide others. Of course, we're never going to be able to hide all of those traits that we deem to be negative because we are human and using an illusion to rate ourselves. The point is that our prism, with all of its various facets, is already perfect. It gives us depth and makes us who we are.

The pressure and stress of creating and maintaining an illusion to hide what we deem as negative is killing us. You can see how this gets projected out into society when we are not tolerant of certain parts of ourselves that do not fit into what we think of as mainstream society. We judge ourselves by what is acceptable…what we look like, what our job is, our net worth, our age, disabilities, performance, religion, gender, abilities, etc. And then we throw in our ego with its faulty belief system and we feel like a hot mess inside. Then we create this same mess on the outside.

Let's take body image for instance. This is a huge problem in our society and so many people struggle with eating disorders especially females. Our beautiful children suffer in silence with this issue. The fear of rejection of withholding love based on one's body shape, looks, color, abilities, wealth, personality or intellect has become a tremendous self-destructive belief for many people. All of the self-destructive behavior is self-rejecting and abandoning and comes from your ego as a cover up so you do not have to feel the pain of your fears, real or imagined.

This needs to stop. We need to teach our children self-love and have them enveloped in a personal relationship with God as young as possible so they know the truth of who they are.

Seeing each of the many facets of our self as being separate and distinct, some of which are good and others bad, causes us to react internally/externally in anger, aggression, judgment, passivity, avoidance, control, self destruction, shame, guilt, passive compliance, anxiety, depression, apathy, etc. We are acting out of the intolerance we have for our own self as being deficient in some way. This is why there is so much hatred and anger in the world.

Too many of us do not accept that we are perfect just the way we are, flaws and all. If we cannot accept our selves how can we accept others or have tolerance for those that we see as being different from us? Instead of projecting our ego's perception of our own ugliness out into the world and then reacting to it, we need to accept the perfection of the diversity.

To add more complexity to this, the prism also contains the past, present and future, and they are all happening simultaneously since there is no such thing as time and space. This is why all of the past hurts feel like they happened just yesterday. It is also why we sometimes get glimpses into the future. I will discuss this more in another volume.

None of us are broken. If you can see this, you have achieved a huge shift in your thinking. We spend so much time outside of ourselves looking to fix our selves or blame others because we are unable to see our own perfection. We try to achieve perfection in the way we look or perform, in how much money or material things we have. We chase the career that will give us status. We look for love and acceptance outside of our selves. Even when we attain high levels of achievement and success we feel as though there is still something missing.

We don't know the truth of who we already are and that nothing is missing. Mind you, this does not mean that we do not work on improving ourselves, learning new things, and striving for health and personal/Spiritual development. Our job is to connect to the highest part of our selves and let this part lead us. This is where our Divine perfection lies, in the God within, and this is the center of our prism, it is our heart.

It is extremely difficult these days to find quiet time with all of the technology, all of the noise around us, the incessant chatter inside us. Modern life connects us to all sorts of information but at the same time it disconnects us from our true selves. If we are unable to connect to our own truth then we can never be connected to anyone else. We become so disconnected from our spirit we can't even see truth.

Of course, our ego believes that it knows the truth,

but it doesn't and never will. What we are feeling is not being connected to God, our selves or anyone, and this feels like sadness, fear, isolation, aloneness, emptiness and grief. This is why we hold onto material things. We collect "stuff", and we collect people. We try to escape and fill the emptiness of our heart with habits and addictions. I have done it all.

Most of the clients and couples I work with suffer from this disconnectedness. It is very lonely and it's a shame because everyone tries so hard to be connected to someone or something. We bend over backwards to make people happy or to fit in so that we can feel love and accepted, but ultimately, we have a fear of intimacy. It is a fear brought about by our failure or inability to connect and trust our selves through God.

We spend so much time guarding and judging our self we don't know how to let our self, God, or anyone else into our hearts and to let others and ourselves off the hook. We do not understand what love truly is. This is all caused by our ego that creates separateness within us, separates us from God and from everything inside and outside of us. It is purposeful in that it is designed to assist our growth but there is no truth to this separation. We are never separate from anything. We are all the same energy and consciousness within and without.

Our souls/spirit are inherently intuitive. When our soul speaks to us we often say that we have a 'gut reaction' to something. Most of us don't listen to our intuition/soul, our own truth, because we don't trust ourselves. We look to others to tell us what is right or wrong, good or bad. Other times we are too stubborn to listen to our inner guidance, or anyone else for that matter.

As humans, we find countless reasons not to become quiet, to go inside our selves and listen to our hearts. We need to become more lighthearted and learn to forgive others for not meeting our unrealistic expectations of perfection and love; that's not their job. It's our job to find the love and perfection within ourselves and then see it in others. Achieving this is a long, drawn-out process and it takes a lot of self-compassion and time.

It is difficult to come to terms with the fact that part of you thinks and feels broken (ego) while another part of you is happy and knows it is just fine (soul/spirit). When we give our ego a voice, we act as if we were broken, or hide the fact that we believe that we're broken. When we live in our ego, all we see is brokenness everywhere. We then contribute to that perception through our own negative thinking and energy. We make the world a self-fulfilling prophecy.

Remember, we are manifesting whatever it is we believe and feel about ourselves. If we think we are broken, we will be. The manifestation of our negative thoughts and feelings is a huge problem. Our ego is always projecting fear, lack, scarcity, victimization, divisiveness, negativity, suffering and brokenness into our lives.

The more work you are able to do to lovingly separate your self from your ego (not listening to it or giving it any power) and see ego for what it really is, the more you will be able to limit all of the negative manifestations around you. If you keep working at it, eventually your positive thinking and creating will take over. This takes enormous self-discipline through deepening a spiritual relationship and healing in a much different way than what we are used to. This isn't the same kind of self-discipline that you need to get up off of the couch to go to the gym or exercise class!

As you are progressing along your path, the changes will be very subtle at first. Even though it may not be readily apparent to you, you are making amazing advances. We are all so programed to only recognize immediate gratification that we don't see the progress we are making over time; but it is happening. The more time you can set aside to be by yourself and integrate all you have learned, you will be amazed by all of the wisdom you have acquired and the positive changes you have already made.

The Prism of Life

In the mirror of life we see the illusion of who we are and it takes time to stop allowing the illusion to define us, for we are all so much more. The illusion we see is of all the fractured broken parts of us that need to be healed, and the parts we deem unworthy. These are the parts that guide our days and nights. Every now and then we see through another lens, another pane of glass in the prism, and we see all the amazing and loving parts of us that are already perfect, it is our soul, our heart. This is a window through which we can see our truth and our divinity. It is our life's journey to take time to look, to explore, to heal wounds, to discover the faulty beliefs and programming and then forgive and let go. We need to embrace the Divine grace and unique facets that live within us. We need to accept, love and have tolerance for the diversity within. This is how we heal the fractured beliefs that keep us separate and move toward the wholeness of our beautiful complex self.

Chapter Fourteen

PROJECTING POSITIVE ENERGY
FOR THE PLANET

*If self-love were inherent in everyone
our planet would look very different.
All souls need to move toward self-love...*

None of us can deny that the external world is in a sad state of affairs. The human condition can be heart-breaking and unfair. Most of the world isn't doing the necessary spiritual work and as a result, ego, greed, fear and hatred are in control. Each day, we witness a collective anger, hatred, and lack of compassion for our selves and others.

Every human being is here to do the same thing, to transcend and evolve her/his soul. Each of us has the same responsibility to do this and each has been given the same Spiritual vortex of love. If we continue to pass on generation after generation of unhealed family anger, victimization, entitlement, hatred, scarcity, fear, struggle, separation, Illusion, and frustration, then we are collectively adding to all the negative energy in the world.

Some people have grown up with more education and more opportunity than others. It is important to help people improve their condition as opposed to pushing them down. We need to pull others up with us. We exert a positive influence by doing our own spiritual work and by creating and passing along love, encouragement and positive energy. If we allow scarcity, discrimination, victimization, entitlement, lack, judgment, anger, and hate to dictate our lives, then that is what we will continue to create for our selves and for others. It is all very divisive.

This is all part of our souls' lessons. We all have the power to heal ourselves by transcending our ego. We recognize that ego will always be a part of us, but we have to refuse to give it power. As we do this we then have power to help others heal and evolve. Our positive energy and our love are contagious and this is how we conquer the ego, evolve it and defuse all the negative energy that followed us here. This is our role as humans, to do our spiritual work, evolve our souls and grow our hearts.

Sometimes we become so upset with the injustice we see that our energy turns negative even though our intentions are in the right place. Since we are projecting all of the unresolved unfairness that we experienced in our life, when we encounter apparent injustice, we react to it with anger, judgment and hatred. All we're really doing is creating more negative energy. What is required is that we react to this perception of injustice and misfortune with compassion and love and have grace by praying for people to heal and attain more light (wisdom). This is accomplished by transforming your own energy to love and joy.

If we are coming from a standpoint of not understanding life and projecting negativity, anger, and frustration, then we are unwittingly participating in the destruction of our selves, others, and the planet. Everything is vibrational energy and then forgiving our selves and others for our lack of understanding can aid in making positive changes.

The ego is ignorant of all things within and without. To expect others to 'just know' what is right or wrong comes from our ego's ignorance. When we expect others to act in certain ways, we believe that we are somehow better than they are, but that really is not the case. No one is better than another. We are all the same. We also do not understand what their journey is about.

Some of us have a little more knowledge, wisdom and resilience. Some of us have better opportunities. It's easy for our ego to give us a feeling that we are entitled, but we are not. It's easy for our ego to make us believe that we understand everything, but we really don't. This is all a lack of maturity, blaming others for our pain and suffering. The ego is extremely immature. The truth is, everything is working perfectly and is in Divine order.

As you grow in understanding, you realize that your soul is already perfect and that as your faith and trust increase, you will be blessed with the abundant life you deserve because you open yourself up to receiving. Your blessing isn't in the future; you have already been blessed. It is a part of your divinity and your journey. You don't need to worry about anything. It is all waiting for you. You simply need to keep digging inside to find it, see it, know it, and then consciously co-create it.

We still have to live in the natural world where we have no control over others, just our selves. If something doesn't work out, then it was not meant to be. If a door closes, another will open. We simply have to be open, patient and willing to receive.

For most of my life I carved out my path with a machete. This took a terrible toll on me; it was very tiring. I forced and pushed my way forward because I did not understand that my path was already laid out and that I had Spiritual support. I just needed to allow myself to be led. As I continued to evolve in trust and as I came into greater alignment with God, I was brought what was meant for me, and the Universe served it to me on a silver platter. It is just coming to me at exactly the right time. That's the origin of these books. Jesus said, "Deb, it is time to write."

Remember, part of evolving is learning to have trust and faith in God and in your self. No dream is too big, so envision and create the life you want. Visualize yourself, centered, evolved, living from your heart, full of love for yourself and others.

Visualize (but not in your ego) how others will feel about you. See how you are expressing your purpose in life, if you can, and how you add to the collective consciousness of the world. What does your life look like? What does a day in your life look like? Remember, life is an illusion and although we have awakened spiritually, it is time to make a new story that is devoid of all the old programming and patterns handed down from the last story. Make this new story a good one!

Continue to dream and create. Hold a vision of your dream and write it down. Set a goal date for when you would like things to happen and use your guidance to help you with this. Although, not everything works on a timeline, we are being prepared for certain dreams to become reality. Hold the vision, but let go of the outcome. Hold the vision in your heart, and allow faith and trust to lead the way. Your vision will manifest when you are ready for it. Include a loving peaceful vision for the planet as well.

Don't consciously try to push your vision forward too quickly. When you do and the time isn't right, you'll get a lot of resistance from the Universe. Your vision will manifest at the most perfect time and it will be amazing. This is what I add to my visions and prayers. They are a mixture of different prayers from people and books I have picked up along the way.

God, please bring me these blessings
Or something better
Under your grace
In your most perfect ways
Let them unfold through joy
With no harm to none.

Chapter Fifteen

HOW DO YOU FIND THE DREAM IN YOUR HEART?

Nurture the peace within you
That is all that matters...

God has placed His covenant in our hearts. His dream and purpose that your soul agreed upon prior to birth is what you are seeking. This is what these books are about. They are a guide to help you understand that this agreement between your soul and God exists and to help ignite your passion to realize the covenant. This only comes from having the desire to seek through your heart. Your dream is connected to your purpose, your calling, and God's will. As you begin to create your new life story, it's necessary to find and include God's covenant that is waiting in your heart.

The Universe that lives in each of us collects all of our

dreams and as we continue to grow and are ready for that dream to manifest, it (the dream) then presents itself. I'll give you some examples from my own life.

As a small child, I often visited my grandparents in Florida, and it always felt like home to me. As a result, when I was a little child it was always a dream of mine to live in Florida. That dream has now come true.

I remember when I was about nine years old I told God that I wanted to be one of his Angels so I could help Him help people. In my late twenties and early thirties, I prayed for five straight years that God would give me direction and show me my life's purpose. I was very unhappy and lost. Then one night, after all those years of praying for direction, I had an incredibly powerful dream that I believe was Divinely inspired. As a result of that dream I did something that no one in my family had ever done, something that my parents told me I wasn't smart enough to do, I enrolled in college with the dream of becoming a therapist.

After a tremendous amount of hard work and sacrifice, that dream came true and I spent several wonderful years helping people and then finally in my own private clinical practice. That's not to say that I accomplished this all on my own. I am so grateful to my amazing former partner, Dr. Nitin Sheth, for his help in my success as a private practitioner. When you bring your passion and purpose into alignment with God's plan for you, the right people will show up in your life.

I also remember watching the television show 'Frazier' and loved his call-in radio show, and seeing Barbara DeAngeles in the early 90's on television talking to a large audience about the power of love in relationships. I remember thinking how cool it would be to have the opportunity to speak to a large audience or to have my own radio show so people could call in and I could help them. I dreamed of being in a position to help greater numbers of people than I was able to do in my clinical practice. I dreamed and I prayed.

In fact, for the past fifteen years or more I prayed to God almost daily to please help me find a way to expand my ability to connect with and help more people. That dream is coming true in my life right now as you are reading this book. I've written three books in the past year. I have expanded my career and given workshops to reach more people. I now have my own radio talk show on AngelHeartRadio.com that broadcasts internationally.

Are you seeing a pattern? I had a dream in my heart and asked for Divine assistance to make that dream come true. Then the dream manifested itself into reality when the time was right.

As I prayed to God, I didn't stipulate how my work should unfold or what it would look like. It's so amazing how God brings us our dreams in the right place and at the right time when we are spiritually ready to live them.

It's a beautiful surprise to see your dreams being manifested, being co-created with God, and seeing that they are so much bigger and better than if you simply planned them out yourself. I did not have to go out and look for them. These things just came to me because I was willing to receive and opportunities presented themselves step by step. I just had to have the courage to say yes. When I was ready, they appeared.

If we get bogged down worrying about when our dreams will manifest and exactly what form they will take, it only creates frustration and struggle, and then we get in our own way. God never forgets our dreams, no matter how old they may be, but we have to be ready to receive, which means we always have to be moving forward in our spiritual growth.

As you meditate or pray, it's important to ask God to show you the dream in your heart, to show you your purpose. Allow God to speak to you through your heart, thoughts, images, inner hearing, dreams or just knowing. Keep focusing until you have your answer. It may not come right away. It may not come all at once. When your dream does appear, you might be surprised to find that it is very different than what you originally thought it would be. So, be prepared for anything.

Once you understand your dream/purpose, you may realize that you have a lot of hard work ahead of you. You might have to go back to school to enhance or acquire some new skill. You might need to become proficient in doing something that has always terrified you before, such as public speaking. That would be me! I joined Toastmasters to help me get over this fear and work on improving my speaking skills and it has helped immensely.

Be open and receptive to what you hear through your heart. Your ego may not agree and become judgmental about your dream/purpose. Your ego may feel threatened when it realizes that achieving your dream will mean ego's loss of control over you. It may fill you with fears and self-doubts. Don't give up. Don't give in.

Just observe the ego and don't let it interfere with your following through. Over time you'll learn to trust your guidance more than your ego. You never have to protect yourself from your guidance, but you'll always need to protect your mind and heart from your ego.

Have you ever had a dream of what you really feel passionate about? Did achieving that dream seem impossible, so you dismissed it and forgot about it? Take out a piece of paper and go back as far as you can remember and write down any memories of dreams that you had in your heart, even if they seem silly to you now. Ask your guidance the truth about these dreams and whether they are in alignment with the higher purpose that God put in your heart and that you agreed upon before you were born.

If you can't find any memories, right now, don't worry, try again later. Your guidance will bring those memories to you when you are ready to know and receive them. Sometimes we think we're ready to receive something and we're anxious and impatient to take the next step, but we're really not quite ready yet. When we're impatient with our journey's progress (or perceived lack thereof) it's a sign that we need a little more grace for our spiritual growth to continue.

Learning how to enjoy the process and not just get to the destination is part of our lessons. It is one that I struggle with myself. I have always been focused on the destination and missed all the life and enjoyment in between. We're always impatient, always pushing the process according to our own time line. Impatience comes from our ego. Breathe, relax, and be patient and forgiving. Your new story is on its way and will show up at just the right time.

If you're not getting answers yet, it's okay. It just means more work needs to be done before it will be revealed to you. Don't become frustrated. We're always trying to push the future for reassurance. We dislike not knowing what will be happening next or not having control over situations. We just need to stay in the present so we can continue to grow. It may be that you're acquiring wisdom that is needed before you can fully understand your purpose. When it is the right time and you have your answer, you will then start to see pieces of it unfolding and the creative process beginning.

When you are trying to manifest and create you need to see yourself living your dreams and having a successful outcome. See your dream and feel it in your heart. Feel the feelings, excitement and gratitude as if it has already happened and then stay in that mindset. It's your heart's desire to express your dream for the greater good...the collective good of all so it is important to co-create with God.

I mentioned earlier my story about being nine years old and telling God that I want to be one of his angels so I could help Him help others. I distinctly remember saying this repeatedly around that age. I remember thinking and feeling that I was a bad girl. I used to lie a lot and was mischievous due to all of the dysfunctional chaos in my home. I told God that I didn't want to be that person anymore.

My experience of God felt fatherly because I needed a strong loving father role model. Our connection with God comes in whatever form we need and whatever form we will accept to help nurture, love and heal us, although, God is energy not form. It is the pure energy of Divine love.

I always knew God was there with me even though I had no formal religious teaching or upbringing. I had an angel with me then who would hold me and comfort me as a child. Over time and growing up in difficult circumstances, I forgot and became disconnected from hearing and seeing my angel.

Even though I had become disconnected, my inner guidance never abandoned me, just as it never abandons you. Even though I had turned away from my knowingness, my intuition caused me to feel that I was still being led by some positive universal energy. I could feel it, like a wind at my back. I didn't trust it though. I thought that I needed to walk my own path.

I didn't reconnect with my spiritual guidance again until I was fifty-six. I could see, hear, and feel Jesus. It was a huge surprise for me that Jesus was my guidance. Being Jewish, I didn't understand how that could be and went through a process of having to undo my societal/religious programing in order to just accept love and not question the source.

Jesus is a master teacher in God's Kingdom/Universe. It is a great comfort to know His love and wisdom. He saved my life. I couldn't imagine going through the rest of my life without Him being with me every moment of every day. I learned that we are all given the love and support we need, and that gift has absolutely nothing to do with religion unless that is the contextual format that works best for you. We are all given divine love and light, and there are many spiritual guides waiting to share love and wisdom with you.

As my own spiritual practice grew through taking a thirty-day course with Margaret Paul to raise my vibration, I was then able to see and hear God/Spirit, my higher self, my older wiser self, Archangel Michael and Gabriel, my father who passed away in 2008, my maternal great-grandmother and others. My guides have been a blessing and have changed my life. I do see all of them as form and I feel their energy. I have come to understand that much of the time; the knowledge and wisdom I learn from them come from a collective Spiritual consciousness. At other times, I am given a direct lesson just from that particular Spirit.

You will feel the same way when you find your spiritual guides, they will know what and when is best for you. With the support you receive you can flourish and become the person you are meant to be. That is your guides' goal for you. Your guides will give you all of the love, direction, reassurance and patience that you need along the way. It's a pity we don't understand that we have access to these gifts all of our lives. But then again, if you truly understood who you are from the very beginning, it would not make your awakening as wonderful an experience as it's going to be.

Chapter Sixteen

PUTTING GOD/SPIRIT FIRST

My heart feels full with God's glory, it is deep within me
It washes over me with peaceful contentment and bliss,
knowing that He is in control of my life,
that I need not worry
And if I should fall, He is always there to catch me,
to lift me up to my highest and bring me out of the dark
which is where my mind tends to go.
He sees the beauty in me when I can no longer see.
I rest my head on His chest and He consoles me
I humbly accept His hand for there is no other love
that can fill as completely and fully
I am your humble servant of love forever more...

Since we are all spiritual beings created from God's love and energy, we all have the same goal of evolving our soul to higher and higher levels of consciousness, and growing and opening our hearts. Putting God first means putting your self first. This is the complete opposite of what most religions or societal programming will tell you. None of the major religious theologies teach that we should put our selves first. That is why most people believe that if we do think about ourselves first, we are being selfish. This idea of selfishness is one of our ego's most powerful tactics to prevent us from caring for our selves spiritually, emotionally and physically.

There are a lot of misconceptions surrounding the concept of putting God first in our lives. Most religions teach that you need to do certain things and live certain ways in order to put God first. This can be very confusing. I am writing from a spiritual standpoint, not religious. We are all spiritual beings first and foremost.

The message I received growing up was that I should not be thinking about myself first, I needed to worry whether my behavior was making other people happy and if I was not acting accordingly, then I was selfish and a bad girl. Most of us have received this message in one form or another. We do need to put our selves first and take good, loving care of ourselves otherwise we are not going to be fully able to give of who we are to anyone or anything else. This does not mean shirking our responsibilities. The most significant part of self-love is connecting with our Divinity.

Let me clarify, God wants what is best for you and knows you better than you know yourself. God and your soul created you (in human form) with a special purpose, gifts, and talents. Unless you develop an intimate relationship with God, with your higher self, you cannot know what is best for you or what you were created to do. You must develop a relationship with God in order to understand that you are completely and unconditionally loved, to recognize who you are, and what your purpose and higher calling is. God holds the keys to unlock everything you need to know about life. If you have a relationship with your higher self it will take you to God. In fact, your higher self is God. There is nothing special that you have to do, or say, or be. All you need to do is open your heart and tell God, or whatever you call the energy of love, that you want a relationship so that you can love your self and fully understand who it is that you truly are. That's it!

Some religions refer to this as surrendering. Most of us don't even think about surrendering until we're completely beaten down, desperate, despairing, and without hope. We've hit rock bottom. We're trapped and see no other way to turn. We surrender.

We don't have to wait to surrender to God until we're filled with misery or illness. Most of us resist the idea of surrendering because our ego believes that by doing so we are giving up our life and our power. There's no truth to this.

It is our ego that fears giving its power to anyone or anything. If you believe there is nothing more powerful than you, that you can find all the answers and figure it all out by yourself, then you are living in your ego. Remember, it's your life's journey to stop living in your ego and get in touch with your higher self.

If you have a sense that you have a higher part of you or know there is a better part of you somewhere deep inside, then you have identified your higher self which is part of your soul. The only way to evolve is to nurture this connection and become one again.

Your higher self/soul is pure love, light, compassion and has great love and regard for you and everything else. It doesn't judge. It is filled with grace and understanding that you are human and asks nothing in return other than you accept all the gifts that are waiting for you with grace. These gifts are love, peace, wisdom, knowledge, truth, abundance, creativity, blessings and miracles. They are wrapped in enough love and patience to allow you to take as much time as you need to understand them and integrate them into your being.

As you work your way through this process of connecting to your highest/soul, you are subtly evolving into who you truly are and are coming into the life and happiness you deserve and were made for. The journey brings you freedom from all worries and fear. Know that you are taken care of forever; you are never alone.

Journal Entry 1/10/2016
With Angel Simon

Simon: *God's purpose is to heal everyone through the blessing of His love and His spiritual kingdom that is always there to help everyone heal. He wants us to receive all that He has given us past, present and future. You are beginning to understand. Now you need to let it sink in as you dwell on this, and allow it to be your own understanding of human life. The goal is to heal your human hurts which allows your soul to evolve to its highest. You are God's progeny.*

Me: *What is progeny?*

Simon: *Lets look it up.*

Me: *(I get told to look up words and concepts all the time) Progeny is a descendent(s) or offspring or offspring collectively. So we are all God's offspring (soul, human life and all that exists) and the meaning of our time on earth is to find God, remember that we are connected to Him, that we are His offspring and that we come back to Him as our parent to heal us by awakening to all the love He is surrounding us with. We have* *to recognize that we have become closed off to our soul/spirit in a kind of a "great sleep". We have to awaken and allow God to re-parent us through His love so that we can mature our divine soul. He is our soul's mom and dad. God's soul (energy) made our soul (energy). Our soul needs to be nourished and that spiritual nourishment can only come from our spiritual parent. So God representing our mother and father is a human way of looking at it. God is both male and female, yin and yang, the flow of energy, the life force and life source.*

Simon: *Yes, very good.*

Me: *So why do I experience God as a male?*

Simon: *Some of it is social context, programing. Some of it is that you needed to heal paternal wounds and remember that even though you received those wounds from your father, you also experienced love from him as well.*

Me: *So, God is experienced through whatever a person needs, whatever a person feels comfortable with?*

Simon: *Yes, but God is neither male nor female; He is energy, He encompasses both masculine and feminine.*

Me: *We all like symbolism, so if I were to see God as energy what would it look like?*

Simon: *It would look like everything. God is your blanket or the TV or your coffee cup, your husband, children and yes, yourself.*

Me: *Wow, that's really a lot to take in.*

Simon: *Symbolism is very important, that is why God sent Jesus, saints, apostles, so that there is a symbolic reference to what God is. Humans relate to symbolism and the symbols are there to remind people to wake up from the great sleep and reconnect to their soul's purpose in life, to mature and grow, just like you do…like a child growing into an adult. But only God can mature and parent your soul.*

Surrender to Happiness

These words flow through me everyday in the most loving ways. I am reminded to feel the fullness of my love and happiness within. It is God's way of bringing us back to the core of who we are. It is a blessing to hear this reminder since our ego keeps trying to diminish what is truly ours. At the core, we are pure joy, nothing else. Look into your own eyes. Look past the surface and see the light that is illuminated within, the eternal light of love and joy that flows through your veins (your being). This light never gets extinguished, although it might be dimmed. By reconnecting to your heart, God will ignite it over and over again as your soul pursues its endless quest to return home to who you truly are, a lighthouse of love, hope and joy.

Chapter Seventeen

WHY DO WE CALL GOD, GOD?

*When the willows blow in the wind
the seeds are carried away and
deposited along the way.
These seeds are new life beginning to take hold
and become a beautiful expression of nature...*

I don't profess to be a student of linguistics. I have made no study of languages and how they have developed and changed over time. I subscribe to a translation of the English word 'God' suggested by Craig Bluemel in his article 'The origin of the English Word for God', Part One, which can be found at Bibleanswerstand.org. Bluemel suggests that the English word 'God' translates from another language where the word means 'good.' The word 'God' stands for 'divine good' or 'involved one."

My definition of the word 'God' for this book is 'divine

being of goodness'. I see God as energy, divine spiritual energy. I think it is easier for others to accept the idea that we are all 'divine beings of goodness', that we are spiritual energy, than it is to understand that we are God, or are one with God, although, that is truth.

The word God means so many different things to different people. It's important to have a definition of God that you're comfortable with. I hope you can see yourself as a divine being of goodness. It's an important concept to grasp as you begin to do this work.

If you consider that the real you is your soul/spirit, the highest part of you, the definition makes sense. It is our ego that doesn't want to accept the word 'God.' Ego thinks of God as having complete control over everyone and everything and, of course, ego doesn't want to relinquish its illusion of control due to fear.

Now we can substitute the idea of 'coming into alignment' for the somewhat more difficult term 'surrender', which for some implies giving up power or control. Alignment means to be in a position of agreement or alliance, hence God's Covenant. When we align ourselves with God, the relationship is mutual, reciprocal; it is not giving your self up. It is pure giving and receiving of love. When Jesus dictated this to me, it was a real epiphany for me...a real 'A-ha' moment.

We have been programmed to believe that surrender has a strong negative connotation. I hope that now you can see that in the spiritual sense, surrendering to God and aligning ourselves with God, is the most positive and natural thing we can do.

It's inspiring to realize that there is a divine being that is mutually interested in our success in all areas of our life. Doesn't it make sense for us to seek out this relationship, to try to align our selves with that being, to align our soul with our soul's parent?

Unfortunately, in our society the very idea of God has taken on a negative connotation to some people. Many people have given up on God because they have suffered disappointments and misery in their lives. If they see God as being 'in control,' they then struggle to understand how a divine being of goodness that is loving, compassionate and in control would allow bad things to happen to them or others.

I wouldn't even know where to begin to try to answer these questions, for I cannot. We do not understand the bigger picture of why we are here. However, if we truly seek, find, and develop an intimate relationship with God we come to understand this relationship and knowledge differently. When we come into alignment and experience a personal relationship with God we understand that God does not turn away from us. It is we who turn away. We run away.

We blame and deny there is such a loving spirit because we don't truly understand the unconditional love, how to access it or know how to receive it. Yet, it is what we all are craving, unconditional love. It is not available outside of us, yet this is where we seek it. We look to other human beings, pets and objects hoping to supply us with never ending unconditional love and happiness. This is just not possible.

God is only interested in a one-on-one relationship with you. It is up to you to do the seeking. That is what your journey on earth is about. God is always present in our hearts. We just need to clear away the clutter to get to it. The more you allow your programing and society's programing to interfere with your journey, the more you lose out on knowing all the love and gifts that are awaiting you, and the gift that you truly are.

This is the hardest work you will ever have to do, but the benefits are priceless. You will keep bumping up against feelings of guilt, and shame, and patterns that act as a wedge keeping you from connecting with God and accepting your worthiness and divinity.

Most of us carry so much guilt and shame as a result of our inherited familial and societal programing, and that includes programing about the concept of sin. If we feel sinful, guilty, or unworthy it keeps us from getting close to God. Remember, we are projecting everything about ourselves onto others, including God. If we are judging our selves unworthy then we are projecting that God will see us that way as well or that I don't believe in myself so

I cannot believe in anything else.

There is no truth to this at all. You are looked upon as holy (sacred) and there is no judgment because there is no such thing as right, wrong, or sin; we are guiltless and innocent. When we believe we are right or better than others we are still judging others on a sin scale. 'I am not as sinful as that one.' This idea or belief about sin will keep you from truly understanding that God does not judge you.

You are holy (sacred) and loved. As you learn to accept God's/Spirit's love, your shame and guilt become less of a barrier to building your intimate relationship with God and the shame and guilt will eventually dissipate. Learning how to receive love is a huge lesson in itself.

Chapter Eighteen

GOD IS HOLY,
GOD IS YOU,
YOU ARE GOD,
YOU ARE HOLY AND SACRED...

Why do we need to bring ourselves
to the brink of devastation
when all we need to do is ask the divine self
that resides within for help?
We already have an internal compass for
every area of our life.
We do not have to wait until
desperation sets in...

We are all sacred divine beings of goodness. It is our ego that believes the opposite. It is easy for the ego to control you if it makes you feel sinful, guilty, or shameful. The ego's job is to get you to fall in line so it can control you and keep you safe. It doesn't understand that you're already safe, and it never will.

Your soul/spirit knows you are safe and holy and that there is no such thing as sin. Our ego believes in sin due to its inherited programming. It creates storylines, dramas, entitlements, self-destructive patterns and all kinds of violence that we act out on others and on our self. It believes we are sinful, and it feels the need to hide our sin or blame our self or others for our sinfulness.

If I told you there is no such thing as sin and that there are just thinking errors and poor judgments based on your ego's irrational perception, would that take away the feeling of guilt, shame and unworthiness?

The truth is, we just make errors in our thoughts or actions as a result of decisions or understandings based on our ego's belief system, which is fear and illusion. If you can accept this as true, it will bring a huge shift in your understanding of life and who you really are. You'll cease carrying around all of that heavy emotional baggage about yourself and others. Remember, all that emotional weight affects us physically, emotionally and spiritually.

We are experiencing a 3D reality yet we are dreaming our life. I know this makes no sense because all of our senses tell us that what we are experiencing is real. If we are dreaming our 3D reality, then anything we have done or experienced that we feel bad about, never really happened. As you come closer to understanding this truth all of the thoughts of sin, guilt, shame and blame start to dissipate.

We need to stop believing in sin. It separates us from our Spirit and from God. Our family/society/religion programed us to believe in the concept of sin and our ego uses it to terrorize us, keep us in line or to act out and blame others. No one is to blame. It's part of your awakening to understand that what you learn in the outside world has little or no truth to it.

If you don't keep digging for answers through a personal relationship with God, you can never learn the truth about anything. It is everyone's job or task to seek truth from within. If you are in alignment with God or are in a mutual relationship of adoration, then healing will come. It is waiting for you to embrace it. It just takes faith and belief.

Imagine how much everyone has suffered by believing they are sinful and that God thinks them unworthy. Our spirit/soul does not sin. It is only our ego that makes errors in judgment and thinking. It's heartbreaking to know that so many of us, including myself, have believed so much un-truth for so long. When I first met God I could not even look Him in the face. I was flooded with guilt, shame and unworthiness. This keeps us in pain, alone, empty and feeling lost.

But we aren't lost. We're just disconnected from the truth because we refuse or don't know how to connect to God; it is like a delusion. When we let go of the delusion of believing the untruth about ourselves we are then healed. Through the awakening process we struggle with letting go of the delusion, it is part of the spiritual journey. Our patterns and ego keep us entrenched in believing the delusion. Even if we get a glimpse of the truth, we forget and believe in the delusion again. This happens over and over and over again until we let go of the delusion once and for all.

Sometimes we would rather believe the worst about our self and others than accept the truth of our perfection. We have accepted society's irrational definition of what perfection is and therefore, we cannot see ourselves as perfect. If we are disconnected from God we are disconnected from our selves. Remember, we are Spirit, we are sacred, and we are one with God. We are pure love energy. This disconnect is the cause of all the grief, suffering and despair that we don't want to feel, see, or know. Yet, it is also the fertile ground and foundation that prepares us for our Spiritual awakening, healing and evolution of our soul.

When we feel disconnected from God, we try to fill ourselves with 'things' from the outside world to fill the void of emptiness within and to distract us and numb us from that pain. We become the living dead, living unfulfilled lives, or making believe we are happy and passionate when we're really filled with despair, aloneness, disconnection, separateness, fear and grief. We're spiritually asleep and unconscious and don't understand what we are doing. We don't have to live unfulfilled, empty, spiritless lives trying to fulfill other people or society's plan for us.

It's time to wake up! Take the chains off and get out of the box of illusion. There are many enlightened souls in this world that have found their way to God and have written books or developed programs to help you. There are many paths to enlightenment, including religion. There is no right or wrong way. Everyone's journey is her/his own. The important thing is to discover what works for you, what you feel comfortable with. The only thing that matters is that you are doing the work and going inside to find truth and developing a Spiritual relationship with your self. If you do this you are building a relationship with God.

There is no perfect way to do this. We are perfect. We are human; we make mistakes. However, there is perfection even within the dichotomy of our spirit and humanity. It's all part of the perfection of God. The perfection of our spirit and humanities dichotomy allows us to understand that love and fear exist side by side in each of us, and it is okay.

The process will not look perfect to you through your ego's eyes. It does not see the contrast as perfection; it only sees fear. Ego will find fault with everything you do. Ego will make you feel as though you will never be good enough. Don't believe it! You are perfect. You are right where you should be. Take life one day at a time, one year at a time. Your spirit will lead the way if you allow it to. Always have hope.

Journal Entry 1/10/2016
With Angel Simon

Simon: *Good Morning my darling. We are here with you. We love you. What is your will today Deb?*

Me: *To do God's will, although my ego says to pack and clean is my will (we were in the midst of moving).*

Simon: *Interesting, I am glad that you can separate them. Today is to be holy.*

Me: *Please clarify, what does that mean?*

Simon: *To stay in God's spirit, to delight in awe of your life and what there is around you, to drink in love and beauty, to bestow your love onto others, to share the scripture of heaven.*

Me: *What is the scripture of heaven?*

Simon: *It is to heal and be blessed through the love of God and all that is His. Everything is His, Debbie. All the people living in the world and everything in it, living and not living, are all one with God. Yes, this includes eternity, past, present and future, the pulse of energy that surrounds everything.*

Me: *This is very deep, can you help me understand and integrate?*

Simon: *It will come in time.*

Me: *So, what I am understanding is that being holy means I need to stay connected to His love and purpose and all that God stands for. This would be having gratitude for the blessings of my life, that I am alive and all the abundance I have. To be happy, joyful and honor everything in my life, including contrast, that there is so much that I have been honored with like God's love, family, friends, career, things, home, nature, myself and the gifts within me.*

Simon: *Yes, that is beautiful!*

I sit with You
in the beauty of this peace and calm.
It is only You that can bring this warmth
of love, trust and truth within me.
I am in awe of the comfort
and the fulfillment of my heart.
Keep me; hold me in your arms,
raise me to heights I have never expected,
within and without.
Allow your love to pour through me
like liquid gold that lights up my spirit
and burns brightly, so
I can be blessed as a lantern to others.

Chapter Nineteen

WHERE SHOULD I BE?

Life is not just something that you experience
It is coursing through every cell in your body.
You are energy. You are life…

There are many levels of awakening and consciousness. Your growth depends on how much time you are willing and able to put into doing your spiritual work. We are all on our own journey and we are not all on the same level of soul maturity, higher consciousness or healing. Remember, we are already healed; we are awakening to the understanding that we need to stop believing the illusion and delusion that we are broken and need to be healed.

If you are reading this, you are already awakened to the truth that there is something more to you, something more to life. You probably don't see it clearly or, if you do, you don't think you are far enough along on your path to consciousness. We all tend to believe that we need to keep moving on to higher levels of consciousness before we have integrated what we've already learned. We all feel that we are not growing fast enough spiritually, which creates a lot of self-imposed pressure on us. This is simply the ego harassing us by telling us that we are not where we should be, even in our Spiritual practice. Our ego is still alive and well, telling us we are flawed and imperfect even in our spiritual search and in quick need of additional healing. We do need to heal from our wounds and our hurts. The ego's deception is having us believe that we are flawed and broken. We are not. There is a difference between feeling the need to be healed and wanting to have more knowledge.

Our ego can't accept that our healing has already occurred and that we are right where we're supposed to be, unflawed and unbroken. Ego can't and won't believe it. It tells us there must be something more we need to do to grow or be healed. This is the delusion, it is very strong and feels very real.

The reality is that you are soul, you are spirit, and you are perfect as you are. Even though we have finally started to awaken from our unconscious story, our ego still has us caught up in our storyline, with all of its negative patterns, delusions and illusions. We have spent years believing these delusions and a ton of emotional energy trying to hide them. It takes a substantial amount of inner work with Spirit to let go of this belief system.

We keep repeating the awakening and healing process and then rejecting the fact that we never needed to be healed in the first place. Then we forget again and our ego takes over and starts the loop all over again, and again, and again. The loop isn't broken until all the wisdom is fully integrated and we understand that we are, always have been, and always will be, fully healed because we are not flawed.

We have trouble accepting that life is an illusion, that we have been asleep and unconscious and living a storyline that we agreed on prior to our birth. It's all so difficult to grasp, because our ego can't make sense of it. It's even harder to hold onto once we've grasped it!

As we engage in our day-to-day lives we are in our illusions and delusions along with everyone else. We are living our lives based on our storyline, like an actor in a play or movie, a character in a book.

Your awakening is recognizing there is no truth to the story. Your past is just a story. It is not who you are. It is a dream. It is a role you have been playing based on your illusion of life, your experiences and programing. It is a dream that is difficult to awaken from. We wake up for a moment and fall back asleep. When we fall back asleep, we keep getting drawn back into believing the illusion. We still believe that we need to be healed. So we keep working diligently seeking deeper levels of healing to fix our flaws because we still believe we are imperfect.

This cycle will continue until you finally understand you are pure spirit/soul. You are not broken and never were; you were just unconsciously creating pain. I still get stuck in this cycle at times; it is a normal progression for those who are seeking.

I have been working a lot on creating and manifesting. The challenge is not to get caught up in the illusion and delusion. What I have realized is that I am already every thing. I have the ability to create whatever I want. However, I often believe that something is blocking me from manifesting. This is the work of my ego, telling me I am stuck and, unfortunately, sometimes I believe it.

We see so much on the internet these days about removing these blockages. The only blockage is that you believe the faulty beliefs and delusion that something is blocking you, or that you are not already whole. 'Whole' means that you are complete and perfect. You have everything within and are connected to the energy, the vibration of God always. This never changes. We are the creator of everything we see and experience. This is a difficult concept to grasp; nevertheless, it is truth.

Journal Entry with Jesus 2/16/2016
I just started writing these books

Jesus: *Tell me what you are thinking.*

Me: *What part of this life is not a dream. Us talking?*

Jesus: *Yes, everything else is not true.*

Me: *So healing me is actually awakening me from the great sleep of illusion?*

Jesus: *Yes, everyone must wake up, but not everyone does.*

Me: *Why not?*

Jesus: *They are not ready, so they will try it again.*

Me: *How many lives have I lived?*

Jesus: *Many, does it matter?*

Me: *Not necessarily, just curious. I felt when I was dancing today that I was actually a dancer in another lifetime.*

Jesus: *You were.*

Me: *Can you tell me what else I did.*

Jesus: *There is so much, you marched for women's rights, rode horses, spun wool. You taught religion.*

Me: *What kind of religion?*

Jesus: *Judaism.*

Me: *Wow, I don't remember any of that and I am terrible with understanding the tenants of being Jewish today.*

Jesus: *Let's get back to what we were talking about, what were you thinking before?*

Me: *That I now realize that everything I've experienced in life, my husband, my children, and what happened when I was younger was simply a dream, and that because there is a certain collective consciousness of souls, we all participate and take part in each other's dreams.*

Jesus: *Yes, we had this discussion before and it was hard to understand.*

Me: *So I did not suffer abuse, it was something I dreamed?*

Jesus: *It was part of the dream you believed was true.*

Me: *So nothing really happened?*

Jesus: *No.*

Me: *That seems crazy! What a waste of time and energy to suffer something like that and then come to understand that it never really happened.*

Jesus: *It is, I agree, but it is part of your soul's lessons. Are you done with suffering?*

Me: *I would very much like to be.*

Jesus: *Good, then we can start with creating the life that you want here on earth!*

Me: *Okay, I would like that. What do we do?*

Jesus: *Stop doing.*

Me: *What do you mean?*

Jesus: *You feel like you need to keep "doing" to make it happen but it is already done.*

Me: *So, I just need to wait for it to start?*

Jesus: *It already has, you have already been noticing all the blessings, they will just continue. Just enjoy it, do the things that you want to do, that you love to do, have fun. Creating should be fun. What do you want to create?*

Me: *Love, peace, beauty, helping people awaken and heal. I thought we were writing a book to help people awaken, love themselves and others, heal what people believe needs to be healed, although my understanding is that nothing is true about that. What an amazing book "Our Illusion"! What about the aches and pains I have?*

Jesus: *Bodies do breakdown Deb, it is part of being human.*

Me: *But what about healing our bodies; why can't that be part of the illusion or use of our power to do it?*

Jesus: *We do have the power to heal ourselves.*

Me: *So how do I get rid of my psoriasis?*

Jesus: *Believe you can.*

Me: *Believe I can? What about my finger, toe, liver, hair?*

Jesus: *Yes, all of it. Believe that you are completely healed, because you are, everything will regenerate to its healthy point in time.*

Me: *I need more help with all of this. I need clarity. I know I need to stop resisting the truth. I remember when you first told me that life was a dream, that I believed things happened to me and that I experienced them fully, and this was so difficult to understand. I felt like it was time to wake up and understand more but I didn't know how to feel about what I was learning. It was very difficult to wrap my head around the idea that all my experiences are like dreams or nightmares, that they didn't really happen, that I don't carry scars that need to be healed, and that there is nothing wrong with me or anyone else other than what we perceive about ourselves. Now I understand why the idea that we are sinless and guiltless is so very important. It would be very difficult to accept that life is filled with such untruth. It would take away the meaning of everything that we work so hard to apply meaning to. So I understand how one can go from the idea that "nothing really matters" when you first begin to see the illusion of life, to the realization that "everything matters", because you now understand the true meaning, purpose and beauty of everything* *that surrounds you and that it is of your own creation. It hurts to know that most of the planet, including myself, does not understand this and they are living in pain rather than bliss. There is so much unnecessary pain everywhere, but I guess it is necessary to learn our souls' lessons. If you do not recognize it is a dream, you hold onto everything as if it is real. What a complexity! So all I have to do is relax and enjoy life. Of course I need to take care of human business because it is how the world works. When I allow my dreams to manifest by creating and believing it helps me achieve the purpose I am here for, to express my love and joy. I realize I needed to wake up from both the nightmarish and the wonderful parts of the dream of my life to discover they are all just stories. I needed to see the beauty in everything, get rid of the old stories, stop listening to my ego, and heal the negative patterns so I can be free to just be love and co-create with God.*

Jesus: *Yes, this is a lifetime of work. It isn't easy to clear out everything you accumulated energetically.*

Me: *I am so grateful for this gift of clarity and light, Jesus.*

This realization brings great freedom and joy. You can finally just be you. You no longer look at yourself or others in the same way as before. You don't need to prove yourself or get approval from the outside world. You don't need to hide your 'sins' or your untruths. You are plugged into the truth of life. You are aligned with God and you understand your purpose and recognize your gifts. You are awake and present and you understand the Spiritual role that the ego plays in your life and what your soul is trying to achieve, returning home to fulfill its covenant with God. You recognize that you are blessed with Spiritual guidance, and that you are always connected.

We are often surprised when we finally recognize what our gifts are. It might be something that you never thought was in you or something you thought you had no skill for. But there it is, and it is Divine.

You no longer feel lost, alone, or full of grief. Your life becomes purposeful and full of light. You want to share this light and purpose with others. It feels right and you are passionate about it. You feel incredibly enthusiastic because it is coming from your heart and it fulfills and nurtures your soul.

Don't question why, what or how. You'll intuitively know that you were meant to share your gifts and your purpose with the rest of the world. You are being called to inspire others. It is what you are here to do. Embrace it. It is a blessing and so are you.

I love you and you are loved.
Perhaps it is love that caused you to open this book.
I hope that these books teach you how to receive the
most profound unconditional love and then how to
give it to yourself and others.

The next part of your spiritual journey
will be found in Volume 3

See you there; I'll be waiting for you
with more love . . . .